To Him be the Glory.

How We Do House Church

The Biblical Doctrines and Convictions *of* **Reformation Fellowship**

Edited by Dale Partridge

RELEARN PRESS
– SEDONA, ARIZONA –

DEDICATION

To the church planters—those who see the Kingdom and, who by God's grace, further its borders through sacrifice, labor, and love. May God bless you and guide you in your ministry.

THIS IS A HANDBOOK

In your hands is a tool—a written resource for house church planters, pastors, members, and visitors. For that reason, do not expect this composition to read like a book. Instead, it is a reference guide of short essays, statements, and doctrines intended to clarify what our network believes and how we operate. When using this as a quick reference guide, look to the Table of Contents to locate specific topics or sections quickly. If you want additional information about the Reformation Fellowship House Church Network, visit our website at ReformationFellowship.org.

WHAT IS REFORMATION FELLOWSHIP?

Many Churches, One Fellowship, No Buildings.

We are an international association of biblical house churches within the historic evangelical and reformed tradition. Each house church within the fellowship is pastored by a graduate of Reformation Seminary and holds to Reformation Fellowship's Statement of Faith, doctrines, and convictions. Furthermore, pastors must sustain an annual affirmation of the fellowship's theological and ecclesiastical positions to maintain good standing and inclusion in the Reformation Fellowship network. For that reason, visitors can expect substantial similarities between our network churches.

Disclosure: *Reformation Fellowship network house churches are independent and autonomous churches who voluntarily associate and cooperate with each other. Reformation Fellowship does not exercise control over individual churches. We encourage you to examine each individual house church and its leadership against the Scriptures before becoming members. If you have questions about a church's status with Reformation Fellowship, please contact us.*

© 2020 by Reformation Fellowship. All rights reserved.
Version 1.2

No portion of this book may be reproduced, stored in a retrieval system, or transmitted in any form or by any means—electronic, mechanical, photocopy, recording, scanning, or other—except for brief quotations in critical reviews or articles, without the prior written permission of the publisher.

Published in Sedona, Arizona, by Relearn Press.
Written and Edited by Dale Partridge and the Reformation Seminary Theological Advisory Board.
Cover Design by Dale Partridge

Scripture taken from the English Standard Version®. Copyright © 2008 by Crossway. Used by permission. All rights reserved.

For information, please contact us through our website at ReformationFellowship.org.

TABLE OF CONTENTS

Preface: Why House Church?	13

SECTION 01: CLARITY

Welcome: Getting Clear	21
Why Church Membership?	25

SECTION 02: STATEMENTS

Statement of Faith	39
Statement on Scripture	47
Statement on the Church	49
Statement on Baptism and Communion	51
Statement on Salvation	53

SECTION 03: DOCTRINES

Introduction	61
Article 01: Church	63
Article 02: Mission	64
Article 03: People	65
Article 04: Evangelism	65
Article 05: Unity	66

Article 06: Meeting 67
Article 07: Worship 69
Article 08: Governance 71
Article 09: Discipline 75
Article 10: Giving 78

SECTION 04: CONVICTIONS

Introduction 83
Article 01: Appointment 85
Article 02: Expository Preaching 86
Article 03: Biblical Theology 87
Article 04: Houses 88
Article 05: Fellowship 89
Article 06: Discipleship 91
Article 07: Outreach 92
Article 08: Guests 94
Article 09: Multiplication 98
Article 10: Planting 100

SECTION 05: FREE-WORSHIP LITURGY

Introduction 105
The Order of Biblical Worship 109

Preface
WHY HOUSE CHURCH?

> *"That there may be no division in the body, but that the members may have the same care for one another. If one member suffers, all suffer together; if one member is honored, all rejoice together. Now you are the body of Christ and individually members of it."*
>
> 1 CORINTHIANS 12:25-27

For centuries, Christians in the West have enjoyed public church assemblies protected by government religious freedom policies. However, over the past 50-60 years, we have seen two growing threats encroach upon the local church that erodes its witness and freedom. The first is internal, while the second is external.

Internally, we're watching many traditional churches homogenize with the culture. In an interest to attract visitors, these churches have attempted to market themselves with rock-concert-style worship services and elaborate productions. Others have added coffee shops, book stores, skate parks, age-segregated children's programs, and a church campus that looks more like a university than a place for Christians to worship God. But, generally speaking, those churches who have taken this approach to ministry have also opted for watered-down doctrine, unclear theological positions, and preaching that aims to entertain rather than mature the congregation in the Word of God.

However, by God's grace, a generation of born-again Christians has begun to seek the Scriptures in search of something more. As they read, they begin to see the rich, deep, bold, intimate, holy, lovestruck, Gospel-focused Christianity of the Early Church. Yet, when comparing the beauty of this potent form of Christianity to the flashy and superficial form of the present age, they are left with nothing more than a painful incongruency. In other words, for many, the westernized church feels miles away from the biblical church. Here, we are ten feet wide but only one inch deep. There, they may only be one foot wide, but they are ten feet deep! Ultimately, for many years now there has been a growing consensus among mature believers that crowds and buildings are not the best producers of the intimate, family-like culture seen in the Scriptures.[1] Many have even described these highly institutionalized churches as "audience Christianity" where they feel like an "inactive spectator" to a weekly Christian conference.

In a very real sense, these churches, in an effort to attract the lost through theatrics and gimmicks, have neglected the very core purpose of the Sunday gathering—the edification of the saints.

To be straightforward, Reformation Fellowship is by

---

1 Brandon J. O'Brien. *The Strategically Small Church: Intimate, Nimble, Authentic, and Effective*, (Bloomington, MN: Bethany House), 2010.

no means anti-traditional church. On the contrary, we greatly appreciate and support the many faithful traditional churches who stand committed to Scripture. However, we do believe the biblical design for the local church is experienced most fruitfully when placed into a more intimate and modest environment—like a home. It is in these smaller, tightly-knit communities that Christians can not only receive doctrinally-sound preaching from biblically qualified elders but can experience a degree of fervent fellowship, one-anothering, and servanthood that's more difficult to attain in a traditional church.

Unfortunately, this internal degradation of the local church is not our only problem. On the outside, the culture is viscously attacking the Church's beliefs, freedoms, and reputation. Consequently, this rising hostility toward Christian values will soon cause many local churches to move away from the government-sanctioned, publicly visible, and more vulnerable expression of church and move toward a more private, concealed, and agile form of Christian assembly. We must remember, historically, Christian persecution has primarily been driven by governments. Sadly, almost every Western church is currently sanctioned by and formally connected to their local, state, or federal government. As the values of the biblical church and the secular government grow further apart, this civil connection will be broken and the underground church will take root. This shift will not be universal but will occur to varying degrees depending on the political environment of a particular country, state, or city.

While the house church may be new to the West, it is not

new to church history. In fact, even today, tens of thousands of Christians gather in house churches worldwide. For instance, current conservative estimates contend that over 17 million Protestant Christians meet in homes in China alone.[2] Having said that, the vast majority of house churches (in America or abroad) are not led by pastors, elders, or deacons who have received formal theological training. As a result, many of these churches lack sound doctrine, ecclesiastical structure, and theological accountability.

For this reason, Reformation Fellowship aims to produce a global network of biblical house churches led by pastors who have been rigorously trained and are committed to the same doctrinal and ecclesiastical standards of any other faithful and historic evangelical church.

FRUITFULNESS FLOWS FROM STRUCTURE

To be clear, there is no one perfect way to conduct the local church meeting. That is, our ministry is not claiming ultimate knowledge or flawless interpretation of the Bible on these matters. But we do have a considerable amount of Scripture available to us for creating biblically accurate Christian gatherings. While many of these ecclesiological doctrines have been buried, forgotten, or carefully cut out of the modern church practice, we feel that unearthing of God's original architecture is essential.

Furthermore, we believe church fruitfulness flows largely from structure. In fact, we believe spiritual fruitfulness can

---

[2] Karrie J. Koesel. *The Rise of a Chinese House Church: The Organizational Weapon.* (The China Quarterly 215, 2013). 572–89. doi:10.1017/S0305741013000684.

be significantly promoted or prevented by structure alone. This principle is demonstrated all around us. For example, biblically structured marriages principally generate spiritually healthy homes. Biblically structured homes generally produce spiritually healthy children. Because we believe that God's Word does not return void (Is. 55:11), we believe those who earnestly seek God's design for the local church will find that it, too, will yield spiritually healthy souls.

Now structure without the Holy Spirit will leave us only with a moral association of infertile people—a gathering of individuals polished in formation but bankrupt in spiritual power. Like all things of the Christian life, "Unless the Lord builds the house those who build it labor in vain." (Ps. 127:1). That is to say, we are not looking to activate orderly house churches who hold a form of godliness without spiritual power. We are looking to help regenerated, devout Christians who are dedicated to the furthering of God's commission, in God's timing, according to God's Word.

As you have likely noticed by the cover of this publication, the content of this handbook is focused on building biblical churches within houses and not buildings. Nevertheless, we do not believe that biblical church is limited to the home. In truth, we believe there are many biblical churches that gather in buildings, public school auditoriums, community centers, and even under trees, beaches, and huts. It is merely our conviction that houses offer a uniquely intimate, financially sustainable, politically free, universally applicable, and spiritually fruitful expression of church that is harder to accomplish in a larger group setting in a commercial location.

> **To say it again, we are arm-in-arm with our Christian brothers who are shepherding faithful traditional churches around the world.**

We hold the same biblical ecclesiology; we're just carrying out these doctrines in a different location. It is our sincere hope that if the Lord is calling you to plant, pastor, or join a biblical house church, whether domestic or international, whether civilly free or greatly persecuted, this handbook and its humble perspective becomes a useful tool for your journey.

SECTION 01: CLARITY

"Scripture, because of its absolute clarity, brings understanding where there is ignorance, order where there is confusion, and light where there is spiritual and moral darkness."

John MacArthur

Welcome

GETTING CLEAR

"But grow in the grace and knowledge of our Lord and Savior Jesus Christ."

2ND PETER 3:18

The longer you follow Christ, the more you will understand His nature. However, this is easier said than done. Our modern culture has created so many different caricatures of Jesus that many have lost the biblical Jesus altogether. Nonetheless, after an honest reading of the Gospels, you quickly learn one truth central to His ministry—He wasn't interested in winning people under false expectations. In fact, Jesus went out of His way to make sure people had a very clear view of how His followers would think, act, and live. He demonstrates this principle in Luke 14:25-30, 33 when He says:

> "Now great crowds accompanied him, and he turned and said to them, "If anyone comes to me and does not hate his own father and mother and wife and children

and brothers and sisters, yes, and even his own life, he cannot be my disciple. Whoever does not bear his own cross and come after me cannot be my disciple. For which of you, desiring to build a tower, does not first sit down and count the cost, whether he has enough to complete it? Otherwise, when he has laid a foundation and is not able to finish, all who see it begin to mock him, saying, 'This man began to build and was not able to finish.'.. So therefore, any one of you who does not renounce all that he has cannot be my disciple."

Jesus was unambiguous about the telling marks of His followers. He didn't sugarcoat the level of commitment or cost involved in following Him, either. Instead, He was upfront and direct. Furthermore, Jesus is not telling people they must do these things if you want to be His follower—no—He's telling people *if you are His follower,* you will do these things. That is, He is not talking primarily about duty, but the production of clear evidence! Nevertheless, what a contrast from many of today's churches who are focused more on comforting people than communicating to them the Bible's expectations for those who follow Christ.

Like Jesus, this booklet is intended to be upfront and direct—to make it clear what it means to join a biblical church—that is—a church who is deeply committed to adhering to the Bible's model for Christian assembly. We believe God is clear and purposeful when it comes to the design and infrastructure of the local church. In fact, the intricate and elaborate instructions for the Old Testament

Tabernacle and Temple are explicit evidence of this truth. God is a God of order, and He is not silent about His expectations for His people. From this place, we must begin—a place that starts not with a goal for size, popularity, or success but with a heart for scriptural accuracy and fruitfulness.

Allow me to clarify with a brief illustration. There's an old phrase that reigns true in the church community—*what you win people with is what you win people to*. That is to say, if a local church wins folks with coffee shops, light-hearted messages, and childcare, then they have, in some sense, won those individuals to those things. This is not sinful but it is extra-biblical. If we want to get back to the basic biblical model, local churches are to win people to three specific things—the Gospel, the Bible, and the covenant people of God.

That is the goal of this handbook. There is no striving to win attendance at any particular Reformation Fellowship church by any special offer or attraction. There is no hope to earn your commitment through a hidden agenda or unclear expectations. To be frank, it is quite the opposite. This document will outline everything from Reformation Fellowship's formal Statement of Faith, our hermeneutic (our process of scriptural interpretation), our view on giving, gender roles, church governance, and more.

Ultimately, this booklet is both a declaration and an introduction to a biblical house church's doctrines, convictions, and order of worship. As you will learn through your review, we are a house church network that loves Christ and His Word. We are a house church network that believes in the authority of Scripture. But most of all, we are a house church network that hopes to be found faithful by the Lord in all we do. However, any local church you are considering will not be a perfect church, but if it is a church that allows the Scriptures to guide its gathering, then exercise your patience as you make your evaluation.

In a world filled with churches who seem spiritually lethargic and lost, watered down and weak, it is our sincere hope to offer you the information required to help you and your family determine if a Reformation Fellowship house church is right for you.

May the Lord lead you in this journey.

Dale Partridge
President, Reformation Seminary

Overview

WHY CHURCH MEMBERSHIP?

*"But now God has set the members, each one
of them, in the body just as He pleased."*

1ˢᵀ CORINTHIANS 12:18

For some, "church membership" can feel like a dirty word. I can hear it now, "Why do I need to commit formally? Can't I just show up?" However, this shouldn't surprise us in our ruggedly individualistic and freedom-focused culture in the West. As you might know, it is not uncommon to find nomad Christians who move from church to church, always avoiding a formal commitment to a body of believers. Even more, these hide-and-seek Christians find themselves dangerously independent, never submitting themselves to the care of elders and never experiencing the beauty of an accountable, dependable, committed Christian community.

I want to initiate this discussion with a question: As a Christian, do you believe that God calls you to help build a healthy local church? To put that differently, do you think God expects you not only to consume but to contribute to the strengthening of your local church? I believe He does (1 Cor. 12:21-26). However, in order for you to invest in a local church, you must first become a committed and participating member of that assembly of believers. But what does that really mean?

Becoming a church member is just another way of saying you have formally committed yourself to a local assembly of Christians who operate as a church according to the Scriptures. This assembly would include regular and consistent gatherings (Acts; 2:40-47; Acts 20:7; 1 Cor. 16:1-2) where believers can receive the teaching of God's Word (1 Tim. 4:13; 2 Tim. 4:2), can serve and edify one another through the proper use of spiritual gifts (Rom. 12:3-8; 1 Cor. 12:4-31; 1 Pet. 4:10-11), engage in biblically ordered Sunday meetings (1 Cor. 14:26-40; 1 Tim 2-3), submit to the care and authority of biblically qualified elders (Heb. 13:7; Heb. 13:17; 1 Thes. 5:12-13; 1 Tim. 5:17-20), participate in the ordinances of baptism and communion (Luke 22:19; Acts 2:38-42), and proclaim the Gospel to those who don't believe (Matt. 28:18-20). In short, you affirm their Statement of Faith, their core theological doctrines, and the way they carry out church gatherings and community.

To attend a local church and refuse to formalize your membership with that body of believers demonstrates an unawareness of what it truly means to be a member of the Body of Christ. But the consequences of this refusal don't end at mere ignorance. This desire for autonomy also detaches us from the many blessings that come from such a commitment. Sadly, in a church culture that gives these benefits freely to anyone who shows up on Sunday, we must be reminded that these spiritual advantages are explicitly reserved for born-again, baptized, committed, submitted, and united members of a local church. I have listed them below for your review:

THE BLESSINGS OF LOCAL CHURCH MEMBERSHIP

1. Regular, reciprocating fellowship.
(Col. 3:16; Acts 2:42-47, Acts 20:7; Heb. 10:24-25)

2. Spiritual warnings and encouragement.
(1 Thes. 5:11; Heb. 10:23-25)

3. Accountability to Scripture.
(Gal. 6:1-5; Col. 3:16; Jam. 5:16; 20; Luke. 17:3)

4. Communion with the saints.
(John 6:53-58; 1 Cor. 10:16; 1 Cor. 11:25-26; Acts 2:42)

5. Use and development of spiritual gifts.
(1 Cor. 12:4-11; Eph. 4:11-16; Rom. 1:11; Rom. 12:3-8)

6. Protection from theological and doctrinal heresy.
(Acts 20:28-29; 2 Tim 4:2; Tit. 1:9; Tit. 1:10-11; 1 John 4:1)

7. Guidance toward holy and righteous living.
(Eph. 4:15; 25; 29 1 John 3:18; 1 Pet. 1:22; Heb. 10:23-25)

8. Spiritual ministering to the family.

(1 Thes. 5:11; Eph. 4:12; 29; 1 Cor. 14:26; Jude 1:20)

9. Giving in support of the Christian ministry.
(Rom. 12:13; Gal. 6:2; Heb. 13:16; Prov. 3:27-28)

10. Support in spiritual, emotional, physical or financial need.
(Rom. 12:10; Gal. 5:13; Col. 3:16; Jam. 5:16)

11. Discipline in times of sin.
(Gal. 6:1; Tit. 3:10-11; Jam. 5:19-20; Luke 17:3-4; 2 Thes. 3:14-15)

12. Equipping for personal ministry.
(Ephesians 4:11-12; Titus 2:1-5;; 1 Peter 4:11; 1 Pet. 4:10)

UNDERSTANDING THE BIBLICAL CHURCH

Jesus Christ has one Church seen in two expressions—local and universal. The first includes professing believers in Jesus Christ, who assemble in a congregation at a particular location on a regular basis, and the second consists of all professing believers in Jesus Christ (past, present, and future) living across the globe.

The New Testament often uses metaphoric language when describing the local church. For example, we see it represented as a body, a family, a building, a bride, a house, and a flock (Rom. 12:4-5; Rev. 21:9; 2 Cor. 6:18; Heb. 3:6; Acts 20:28). In these metaphors, it's made clear that God's people are not random, independent parts but a collected and identified group—we are "a flock" or "a building" or "a body". That is, the Bible does not imply we are only parts but also a whole. Namely, we are not a mixed bunch of goats, sheep, stones, rocks, arms, and feet—we are a pure and unified unit of one shared identity. Furthermore, if the Good Shepherd knows His flock and His sheep know His voice (John 10:27), it's only fair to assume His undershepherds (pastors) would know which sheep are under their care and protection. Furthermore, it's also fair to assume, like their relationship to Christ, the sheep of a local flock are clear who is spiritually guiding, feeding, and protecting their welfare (Acts 20:28; 1 Peter 5:1-4).[1]

While these God-appointed local church shepherds are by no means the Chief Shepherd, they are, according to Scripture, to mimic Him. Charles Spurgeon once preached in relationship to this truth, "When a local church functions under a biblical order if one sheep strays from the flock their absence will not go unnoticed—the shepherd[s] of that congregation will take note and labor to restore the sheep with great hope (Matthew 18:12-13)."[2]

As mentioned above, the church is also seen as a building where each Christian is a living stone—each stone has a definite place and is not disjointed or in part-time use (1 Pet. 2:5). Charles Spurgeon beautifully affirms this metaphor, too, when he said, "Christian, you are a brick. What is the brick made for? It's made to build a house."[3] The Apostle Paul also

---

1 Donald S. Whitney, *Spiritual Disciplines Within the Church*, (Chicago: Moody, 1996).
2 Charles Spurgeon, *Metropolitan Tabernacle Pulpit Volume 35*, (New York: Pilgrim Publishing, 1975).
3 Tom Carter, *Charles Spurgeon at His Best*, (Grand Rapids, MI: Baker, 1988), 34.

upholds this imagery when he tells us that the Church is "Built on the foundation of the apostles and prophets, Christ Jesus himself being the cornerstone..." (Eph. 2:20). Essentially, we are God's building—His temple—not made of perishable material but hewn stones established and placed by our confession of the Lord Jesus Christ (1 Cor. 3:9-11; 12:18).

But most notably, the Bible describes the Church (and the local church) as a body (1 Cor. 12:12-3; Rom. 12:4-5; Eph. 4:16; Col. 1:18). As you well know, your body is not a loose, disconnected arrangement of parts. You don't have fingers in San Francisco and your feet in Finland. Your body is separated, it's indivisible and joined together. When your foot is injured, your hands come to the rescue. When your wound is healed, your body rejoices as one. Basically, when you become a Christian, you join the universal Body of Christ. When you become a member of a local church, you apply and walk out that universal union with those Christians who are part of that local body. In short, you show that even though you are an individual under Christ's overall headship, you are also a connected member of the Body of Christ locally. It is in this physical and visual display that believers can unify under the ecclesiastical structure, authority, and commitments of Christ and His Word.

SALVATION VS. MEMBERSHIP

As stated above, when an individual is saved, he or she becomes a member of the Body of Christ (1 Cor. 12:13). Because they are united to Christ and the other members of the body in this way, they are, therefore, qualified to become a member of a local expression of that universal Body.

However, the Scriptures offer a variety of additional, post-born-again conditions for those establishing and maintaining "membership" or a committed standing in the local church. For example, in the New Testament, we see a wide range of roles, responsibilities, moral standards, behavioral expectations, beliefs, processes, and guiding principles to be carried out by those who claim the name of Christ. In fact, those who, after deliberate and consistent correction, refuse to adhere to these biblical standards are called to be removed from the local church (Matt. 18:15-20; 1 Cor. 5:9-13). Now, removal from the local church is by no means a removal of salvation. However, in time, their removal may prove to reveal they were never truly saved. That said, it does illustrate the dichotomy of these two realities.

This consistent pattern of local church order and local church commitment continues throughout the Scriptures and is nurtured and protected by those who the Bible calls elders and deacons (a.k.a. appointed pastors and commissioned servants of the local church). Through these two church offices, qualified men shepherd members toward biblical truth, protect members against false doctrine (1 Tim. 3; Titus 1:5-16; Heb. 13:17; 1 Pet. 5:1-4), and serve members according to their needs. Also, the Bible implies that elders, in particular, oversee the processes for formal church discipline, expository preaching, correcting false doctrine, management of congregational giving, monitoring spiritual duties, maintaining unity within the assembly, and more.

CONCLUSION

Ultimately, this sense of detailed infrastructure affirms God's desire for an orderly and cohesive church (1 Cor. 14:33). I believe A.W. Tozer pointed out that God's people have always been thoroughly organized. Consider the Israelites and their 613 laws, which brought order to just about everything they did. Consider the placement of Old Testament elders over the people in numerical step (Exod. 18:13-27). Consider the Levitical priesthood by which they facilitated spiritual duties. Consider the Prophets, the Apostles, and even the early church fathers who brought safety to God's people through humble rule and regulation. As nature declares, God is a God of order, and His Church is no different.[4]

Dr. John Muether eloquently reminds us, "A child without a family is an orphan to be pitied. A man without a country is a refugee to be welcomed. And a Christian without a church is a sheep to be concerned."[5] For anyone who has studied church history, it becomes clear when a person is born into the family God, they want to gather with the people of God. R.B. Kuiper said it best when he wrote, "The Scriptural rule is that while membership is not a prerequisite for salvation, it is a necessary consequence of salvation."[6] The narrative of the New Testament confirms this—Christians are born-again, baptized, and joined together (Acts 2:41-47).

In summary, there is no direct biblical reference for church membership, but it is the indirect biblical principle

---

4 A.W. Tozer, *Church*, (Camp Hills, PA: Wingspread, 2019).
5 John Muether, "Tabletalk Magazine," *Knowing His Voice*, (March 2009): 15.
6 R.B.. Kuiper, *The Glorious Body of Christ*, (Grand Rapids: Eerdmans, 1996), 112-113.

seen throughout the New Testament. Essentially, when you come to faith in Christ, you also enter into a covenant with His Church. That is, as a member of God's people, you should willingly commit *and* submit to God's biblical order for His people. This doesn't mean that you're committed to a particular local church for life, but it does mean you're openly and publicly stating that "Until the Lord leads me otherwise, I'm a part of this local church, the people at this local church are my brothers and sisters in Christ, this man is my pastor, these elders are my spiritual guides, and I will serve Christ together with this body, I will contribute to the financial support of this ministry, and I am willing to be in a reciprocating biblical relationship with those in this flock." When the onlooking world sees this level of unity, dependability, intimacy, love, and connection, the local church becomes a local witness to the power of the Gospel of Jesus Christ.

SECTION 02: STATEMENTS

"The 1689 [Confession of Faith] is the most excellent epitome of the things most surely believed among us. It is an excellent, though not inspired, expression of the teaching of those Holy Scriptures by which all confessions are to be measured.

Charles Spurgeon

Statements
OUR CONFESSION

These Statements on Faith, Scripture, The Church, Baptism & Communion, and Salvation are not originally written content but adapted and/or modernized summaries of doctrinal positions of the 1689 London Baptist Confession of Faith.

INTRODUCTION: The Statement of Faith of Reformation Fellowship (The 1689 London Baptist Confession of Faith and the summarized form found within this document) is reaffirmed annually by the Board of Directors, theological advisors, faculty, and staff of Reformation Seminary. This statement provides a summary of biblical doctrine that is consistent with historic evangelical Christianity. Additionally, this statement reaffirms many of the doctrinal positions of the common orthodox Christian confessions and creeds and identifies our network not only with the Scriptures but also with the reformers and the evangelical church of our modern era.

Historical creeds and confessions affirmed by Reformation Fellowship include the following: The Apostles' Creed, The Nicene Creed, The Chalcedonian Definition, and The

1689 London Baptist Confession of Faith. However, while Reformation Fellowship is firmly and fundamentally of the Reformed Baptist conviction, the network does permit house churches of the Presbyterian conviction within our network if the elders of those churches affirm and hold to the Westminster Confession of Faith. These churches will be clearly identified as "Presbyterian" in their network listing.

Our Summarized
STATEMENT OF FAITH

OF THE 1689 L.B.C.F.

We believe the Bible is the final standard of faith and practice for the believer in Jesus Christ and for His Church. While recognizing the historical, interpretive, and guiding value of creeds and confessions of faith made throughout the history of the Church, we affirm the Bible alone as the infallible and final authority in the life of a believer.

Below is an abridged version of the 1689 Confession for your reading convenience.[1] You can read a complete version of this confession by visiting our website at Reformation-Fellowship.org/1689.

---

[1] This summary of the 1689 L.B.C.F. was originally compiled by the International Fellowship of Reformed Baptists. It has been reproduced by Reformation Fellowship with additions, modifications, and Scripture references to offer greater doctrinal clarity.

1. WE BELIEVE in the one true and living God, in three Persons: the Father, the Son and the Holy Spirit, who is invisible, personal, omnipresent, eternal, dependent on none, unchanging, truthful, trustworthy, almighty, sovereign, omniscient, righteous, holy, good, loving, merciful, long-suffering and gracious.

1 Cor. 8:4,6; Deut. 6:4; Jer. 10:10; Isa. 48:12; Exod. 3:14; John 4:24; 1 Tim. 1:17; Deut. 4:15–16; Mal. 3:6; 1 Kings 8:27; Jer. 23:23; Ps. 90:2; Gen. 17:1; Isa. 6:3; Ps. 115:3; Isa. 46:10; Prov. 16:4; Rom. 11:36; Exod. 34:6–7; Heb. 11:6; Neh. 9:32–33; Ps. 5:5–6; Exod. 34:7; Nahum 1:2–3; 1 John 5:7; Matt. 28:19; 2 Cor. 13:14; Exod. 3:14; John 14:11; I Cor. 8:6; John 1:14,18; John 15:26; Gal. 4:6.

2. WE BELIEVE that Almighty God has revealed all that is necessary to life and salvation in the sixty six books of Holy Scripture which are the Word of God. All Scripture was given by inspiration of God, is infallible and inerrant, and is the final arbiter in all disputes. Its authority is derived from its Author and not from the opinions of men.

2 Tim. 3:15-17; Heb. 4:12; 2 Pet. 1:19-21; Rom 15:4; John 17:17; Matt. 4:4; Ps. 119:160; Isaiah 40:8; Matt. 24:35; Luke 24:44.

3. WE BELIEVE that God made our first father Adam perfect, holy and upright. He was appointed representative and head of the human race thereby exposing all his offspring to the effects of his obedience or disobedience to God's commands.

Gen 1:31, 3:12,13; Rom. 5:12-21.

4. WE BELIEVE that Adam fell from his original righteousness into sin and brought upon himself and all his offspring physical and spiritual death, condemnation and sinnership.

Gen. 3:6, 17-19; Rom. 5:12, 19; 1 Cor. 15:21-22; James 1:15, Ps. 51:15; Isaiah 59:2; Eph. 2:1-3; Rom. 7:9-11; Job 15:14; John 3:6.

5. WE BELIEVE it is utterly beyond the power of spiritually dead and fallen man to love God, to keep His laws, to effectually understand the Gospel, to genuinely repent of sin, or produce saving faith in Christ.

Eph. 2:1-3; 1 Cor. 2:14; Rom. 8:7, Eph. 4:18; Rom. 3:10-18, 23.

6. WE BELIEVE that God, before the foundation of the world, for His own glory did elect an innumerable host of men and women to eternal life as an act of free and sovereign grace. This election was in no way dependent upon His foresight of human faith, decision, works or merit.

Eph. 1:4-5; 2 Tim. 1:9; Rom. 8:28-30; Matt. 25:34; Rev. 13:8; John 15:16; Tit. 1:1-2; Rom. 9:23-24, 2 Thess. 2:13.

7. WE BELIEVE that God sent His Son into the world, conceived of the virgin Mary by the Holy Spirit, unchangeably sinless, both God and man, born under the Law, to live a perfect life of righteousness, on behalf of all who will believe in His name.

Isa. 7:14; Matt. 1:18-25; Gal. 4:4; Luke 1:34-35; John 3:16; 1 John

4:9-10; Rom. 8:32; John 3:15; John 11:25-26; 1 John 3:5; 2 Cor. 5:21; 1 Pet. 2:22; Heb. 4:15.

8. WE BELIEVE that God's Son died at Calvary to effect propitiation, reconciliation, redemption and atonement for His chosen people. God bore testimony to His acceptance of His Son's work by raising Him from the dead.

Rom. 5:8; 1 Pet. 2:24-25; Gal. 2:20; 1 Cor. 1:18-22; Col. 2:14; John 19:30; 1 John 2:2; Gal. 3:13; Mark 10:45; Rom. 10:9; 1 Pet. 1:3; 1 Thes. 4:14; 1 Cor. 15.

9. WE BELIEVE that God's Son ascended to the right hand of His Father and is enthroned in glory, where He intercedes on behalf of His people and rules over all things for their sake.

Acts 2:33, 5:31; Mark 16:19; 1 Pet. 3:22; Eph. 1:20-23; Rom. 8:27, 34; Heb. 7:25; Col. 2:10; Phil. 2:9-11.

10. WE BELIEVE that God the Son has poured out the Holy Spirit to work alongside the preached Word. The Spirit of God regenerates the elect sinner and draws him irresistibly to faith in Christ the Savior.

John 14:26; 16, 15:26; 1 Cor. 2:10-13, 6:19; 1 Pet. 1:12; 1 Thes. 4:8; Rom. 10:17; 2 Thess. 2:13-14; James 1:18; John 3:8; 1:13; 3:5, 6:37; 1 Pet. 1:23; Eph. 2:8; Acts 16:14.

11. WE BELIEVE the elect, who are called by grace, are justified in the sight of God on account of the imputed righteousness of Jesus Christ which is received by faith alone.

2 Cor. 5:21; Rom. 8:29-30, 4:5, 1:7, 3:21-22, 10:4; Phil. 3:9; 1 Cor. 1:30; 1 Pet. 2:24.

12. WE BELIEVE that all who are regenerated, called and justified shall persevere in holiness and never finally fall away.

Phil. 1:6; John 10:27-28; 1 Pet. 1:5; 2 Tim. 1:12; Romans 11:29; Jude 1:24; Rom. 8:30.

13. WE BELIEVE that the moral law of God is summarized in the Ten Commandments and that all the Ten Commandments continue today to be the standard of righteousness which every child of God ought to love and obey.

Ex. 20:1-17; Romans 13:8–10; James 2:8, 10–12; James 2:10, 11; Matthew 5:17–19; Romans 3:31.

14. WE BELIEVE God has particularly appointed one day in seven for a Sabbath to be kept holy unto Him, which from the beginning of the world to the Resurrection of Christ, was the last day of the week; and from the resurrection of Christ, was changed into the first day of the week which is called the Lord's Day; and is to be continued to the end of the world as the Christian Sabbath; the observation of the last day of the week being abolished.

Ex. 20:8; 1 Cor. 16:1, 2; Acts 20:7; Rev. 1:10, Col. 2:16, Heb. 4:9-11.

15. WE BELIEVE that baptism by immersion and the Lord's Supper are gospel ordinances belonging only to regenerated believers.

Romans 6:3–5; Col. 2:12; Galatians 3:27; Mark 1:4; Acts 22:16; Romans 6:4, Mark 16:16; Acts 8:36, 37; Acts 2:41; Acts 8:12; Acts 18:8; Matthew 28:19, 20; Acts 8:38; Matthew 3:16; John 3:23; 1 Corinthians 11:23–26; 1 Corinthians 10:16, 17, 2; 2 Corinthians 6:14, 15; 1 Corinthians 11:26, 29; Matthew 7:6.

16. WE BELIEVE marriage is only to be between one man and one woman and that marriage was ordained by God and, therefore, cannot be redefined by man.

Gen. 2:24; Mal. 2:15; Matt. 19:5-6; Gen 2:18; 1 Cor. 7:2, 9; Eph. 5:22-33; Mark 10:6-9; Heb. 13:4.

17. WE BELIEVE that our corporate worship must be regulated by the Scriptures alone and that we are not free to impose extra-biblical elements into our worship before God.

John 4:21-24; Col. 2:23; 1 Cor. 14:26-40; 1 Tim. 4:13; 2 Tim 2:4; Eph. 5:19.

18. WE BELIEVE that the Scriptures teach that only men—biblically qualified men—are to hold the only two offices Christ has given to the Church, that being elder and deacon.

1 Tim. 3:1-13, 5:17; Acts 14:23, 20:17, 28; Titus 1:5-7; Phil. 1:1; 1 Pet. 5:1-2; Heb. 13:17.

19. WE BELIEVE that the local church is under the authority of Christ alone and not the civil government. Nevertheless, civil authorities are established by God and

Christians should submit in the Lord to them to the extent that their submission does not cause them to disobey God.

Eph. 1:22, 5:23; Col. 1:18; Rom. 13:1-7; 1 Pet. 2:17; 1 Tim 2:1-2; Acts 5:29.

20. WE BELIEVE that the Lord Jesus Christ shall come again to raise the dead, both righteous and unrighteous, and that the righteous shall enjoy everlasting life and the wicked endure everlasting punishment.

Heb. 9:28; 1 Thess. 4:16-17; 2 Peter 3:10; Acts 17:31; John 5:22, 27; 1 Corinthians 6:3; Jude 6; 2 Corinthians 5:10; Ecclesiastes 12:14; Matthew 12:36; Romans 14:10, 12; Matthew 25:32–46.

Our Precise
STATEMENT ON SCRIPTURE

WE BELIEVE that God has revealed Himself and His truth by both general and special revelation. General revelation displays His existence, power, providence, moral standard, patience, goodness, and glory; special revelation manifests His triune nature and His plan of redemption through Messiah for humanity. This special revelation has been given in two ways, preeminently in the incarnate Word of God—Jesus Christ, and in the inscripturated Word of God—the Bible. We affirm that the sixty-six books of the Bible are the written Word of God given by the Holy Spirit and are the complete and final canonical revelation of God for all time. (Rom. 1:18-2:4; 2:14-16; Ps. 19; Acts 14:15-17; 17:22-31; John 1:1- 18; 1 Thess. 2:13; Heb. 1:1-2; 4:12)

WE BELIEVE these books were written by a process of dual authorship in which the Holy Spirit so moved the human authors that, through their individual personalities and styles, they composed and recorded God's Word which is inerrant.

These books, constituting the written Word of God, convey objective truth and are the believer's only infallible rule of faith and practice. (2 Tim. 3:16-17; 2 Pet. 1:19-20; John 10:35; 17:17; 1 Cor. 2:10-13)

WE BELIEVE that, whereas there may be several applications of any given passage of Scripture, there is but one true interpretation. The meaning of Scripture is to be found as one diligently applies the literal grammatical-historical method of interpretation under the enlightenment of the Holy Spirit (John 7:17; 16:12-15; 1 Cor. 2:7-15; 1 John 2:20). It is the responsibility of believers to ascertain carefully the true intent and meaning of Scripture, recognizing that proper application is binding on all generations. Yet the truth of Scripture stands in judgment of men; never do men stand in judgment of it.

Our Precise
STATEMENT ON THE CHURCH

WE BELIEVE the Church is the elect people of God, existing from the beginning of the world and completed at the return of Christ who is its head. The mission of the Church is to glorify God by worshiping corporately, building itself up as a loving, faithful community by instruction of the Word, observing baptism and communion, embracing the doctrinal mandates of the apostles, communicating the Gospel and making disciples of all peoples. (Matt. 16:18; 28:16-20; Acts 1:4, 5; 11:15; 2:46, 47; 1 Cor. 12:13; Rom. 12:4-21; Eph. 1:22, 23; 2:19-22; 3:4-6; 5:25-27; Col. 1:18; Rev. 5:9)

WE BELIEVE Christians should gather together in local assemblies. They are priests before God and to one another, responsible to serve God and minister to each other. The biblically designated officers serving under Christ and leading the assembly are elders and deacons. Although church and state are distinct institutions, believers are to submit to the government within the limits of God's Word.

(Matt. 18:15-18; 22:15-22; 28:19; Acts 2:41, 42; 6:1-6; 1 Cor. 14:40; Eph. 4:11, 12; 1 Tim. 3:1-13; Tit. 1:5-9; Heb. 10:25; 1 Pet. 2:5-10, 13-17; 5:1-5)

Our Precise
STATEMENT ON BAPTISM AND COMMUNION

WE BELIEVE that baptism is an ordinance of the Lord by which those who have repented and come to faith express their union with Christ in His death and resurrection, by being immersed in water in the name of the Father and the Son and the Holy Spirit. It is a sign of belonging to the people of God, and an emblem of burial and cleansing, signifying death to the old life of unbelief, and purification from the pollution of sin.[1] (Matt. 28:16-20; Acts 2:41; 10:47-48; Rom. 6:1-6)

---

[1] While Reformation Fellowship is firmly and fundamentally of the Reformed Baptist conviction, the network does permit house churches of the Presbyterian conviction and, thereby the paedobaptist position, within our network if the elders of those churches affirm and hold to the Westminster Confession of Faith. These churches will be clearly identified as "Presbyterian" in their network listing.

We believe that the Lord's Supper is an ordinance of the Lord in which gathered believers eat bread, signifying Christ's body given for His people, and drink the cup of the Lord, signifying the New Covenant in Christ's blood. We do this in remembrance of the Lord, and thus proclaim His death until He comes. This ordinance portrays His death, the uniting of believers in fellowship, and anticipates their participation in the marriage supper of the Lamb. Those who eat and drink in a worthy manner partake of Christ's body and blood, not physically, but spiritually, in that, by faith, they are nourished with the benefits He obtained through His death, and thus grow in grace. (Luke 22:19, 20; 1 Cor. 10:16-18; 11:23-29; Acts 3:21; Luke 24:6, 39)

Our Precise
STATEMENT ON SALVATION

WE BELIEVE that salvation is wholly of God by grace on the basis of the redemption of Jesus Christ, the merit of His shed blood, and not on the basis of human merit or works (John 1:12; Eph. 1:7; 2:8-10; 1 Pet. 1:18-19).

WE BELIEVE that regeneration is a supernatural work of the Holy Spirit by which the divine nature and divine life are given (John 3:3-7; Tit. 3:5). It is instantaneous and is accomplished solely by the power of the Holy Spirit through the instrumentality of the Word of God (John 5:24) when the repentant sinner, as enabled by the Holy Spirit, responds in faith to the divine provision of salvation. Genuine regeneration is manifested by fruits worthy of repentance as demonstrated in righteous attitudes and conduct. Good works are the proper evidence and fruit of regeneration (1 Cor. 6:19-20; Eph. 2:10), and will be experienced to the extent that the believer submits to the control of the Holy Spirit in his or her life through faithful obedience to the Word of God (Ephesians 5:17-21; Phil. 2:12b; Col. 3:16; 2 Pet. 1:4-10). This obedience causes the believer to be increasingly conformed to the image of our Lord Jesus Christ (2 Cor. 3:18). Such a conformity is climaxed in the believer's glorification at Christ's coming (Rom. 8:17; 2 Pet. 1:4; 1 John 3:2-3).

WE BELIEVE that election is the act of God by which, before the foundation of the world, He chose in Christ those whom He graciously regenerates, saves, and sanctifies (Rom. 8:28-30; Eph. 1:4-11; 2 Thess. 2:13; 2 Tim. 2:10; 1 Pet. 1:1-2). We teach that sovereign election does not contradict or negate the responsibility of man to repent and trust Christ as Savior and Lord (Ezek. 18:23, 32; 33:11; John 3:18-19, 36; 5:40; Rom. 9:22-23; 2 Thess. 2:10-12; Rev. 22:17). Nevertheless, since sovereign grace includes the means of receiving the gift of salvation as well as the gift itself, sovereign election will result in what God determines. All whom the Father calls to Himself will come in faith, and all who come in faith the Father will receive (John 6:37-40, 44; Acts 13:48; James 4:8).

WE BELIEVE that the unmerited favor that God grants to totally depraved sinners is not related to any initiative of their own part or to God's anticipation of what they might do by their own will, but is solely of His sovereign grace and mercy (Eph. 1:4-7; Tit. 3:4-7; 1 Pet. 1:2).

WE BELIEVE that election should not be looked upon as

based merely on abstract sovereignty. God is truly sovereign, but He exercises this sovereignty in harmony with His other attributes, especially His omniscience, justice, holiness, wisdom, grace, and love (Rom. 9:11-16). This sovereignty will always exalt the will of God in a manner totally consistent with His character as revealed in the life of our Lord Jesus Christ (Matt. 11:25-28; 2 Tim. 1:9).

WE BELIEVE that justification before God is an act of God (Rom. 8:33) by which He declares righteous those who, through faith in Christ, repent of their sins (Luke 13:3; Acts 2:38; 3:19; 11:18; Rom. 2:4; 2 Cor. 7:10; Isa. 55:6-7) and confess Him as sovereign Lord (Rom. 10:9-10; 1 Cor. 12:3; 2 Cor. 4:5; Phil. 2:11). This righteousness is apart from any virtue or work of man (Rom. 3:20; 4:6) and involves the imputation of our sins to Christ (Col. 2:14; 1 Pet. 2:24) and the imputation of Christ's righteousness to us (1 Cor. 1:30; 2 Cor. 5:21). By this means God is enabled to "be just and the justifier of the one who has faith in Jesus" (Rom. 3:26).

WE BELIEVE that every believer is sanctified (set apart) unto God by justification and is therefore declared to be holy and is therefore identified as a saint. This sanctification is positional and instantaneous and should not be confused with progressive sanctification. This sanctification has to do with the believer's standing, not his present walk or condition (Acts 20:32; 1 Cor. 1:2, 30; 6:11; 2 Thess. 2:13; Heb. 2:11; 3:1; 10:10, 14; 13:12; 1 Pet. 1:2).

We believe that there is also, by the work of the Holy Spirit, a progressive sanctification by which the state of the believer is brought closer to the standing the believer positionally enjoys through justification. Through obedience to the Word of God and the empowering of the Holy Spirit, the believer is able to live a life of increasing holiness in conformity to the will of God, becoming more and more like our Lord Jesus Christ (John 17:17, 19; Rom. 6:1-22; 2 Cor. 3:18; 1 Thess. 4:3-4; 5:23).

In this respect, we teach that every saved person is involved in a daily conflict—the new creation in Christ doing battle against the flesh—but adequate provision is made for victory through the power of the indwelling Holy Spirit. The struggle nevertheless stays with the believer all through this earthly life and is never completely ended. All claims to the eradication of sin in this life are unscriptural. Eradication of sin is not possible, but the Holy Spirit does provide for victory over sin (Gal. 5:16-25; Eph. 4:22-24; Phil. 3:12; Col. 3:9-10; 1 Pet. 1:14-16; 1 John 3:5-9).

We believe that all the redeemed, once saved, are kept by God's power and are thus secure in Christ forever (John 5:24; 6:37-40; 10:27-30; Rom. 5:9-10; 8:1, 31-39; 1 Cor. 1:4-8; Eph. 4:30; Heb. 7:25; 13:5; 1 Pet. 1:5; Jude 24).

We believe that it is the privilege of believers to rejoice in the assurance of their salvation through the testimony of God's Word, which, however, clearly forbids the use of Christian liberty as an occasion for sinful living and carnality

(Rom. 6:15-22; 13:13-14; Gal. 5:13, 25-26; Tit. 2:11-14).

WE BELIEVE that separation from sin is clearly called for throughout the Old and New Testaments, and that the Scriptures clearly indicate that in the last days apostasy and worldliness shall increase (2 Cor. 6:14-7:1; 2 Tim. 3:1-5).

WE BELIEVE that, out of deep gratitude for the undeserved grace of God granted to us, and because our glorious God is so worthy of our total consecration, all the saved should live in such a manner as to demonstrate our adoring love to God and so as not to bring reproach upon our Lord and Savior. We also believe that separation from all religious apostasy and worldly and sinful practices is commanded of us by God (Rom. 12:1-2, 1 Cor. 5:9-13; 2 Cor. 6:14-7:1; 1 John 2:15-17; 2 John 9-11).

WE BELIEVE that believers should be separated unto our Lord Jesus Christ (2 Thess. 1:11-12; Heb. 12:1-2) and affirm that the Christian life is a life of obedient righteousness that reflects the teaching of the Beatitudes (Matt. 5:2-12) and a continual pursuit of holiness (Rom. 12:1-2; 2 Cor. 7:1; Heb. 12:14; Tit. 2:11-14; 1 John 3:1-10).[1]

---

[1] This *Precise Statement on Salvation* was originally produced by the elders at Grace Community Church in Sun Valley, CA under John MacArthur. It has been adapted and reproduced here by Reformation Fellowship.

SECTION 03: DOCTRINES

"Let it be said emphatically, the church is where the truth is. Sound doctrine always has been, is today, and ever will be the foremost mark of the true church."

R.B. Kuiper

Introduction
CHURCH DOCTRINES

> *"Till I come, give attention to reading, to exhortation, to doctrine."*
>
> 1ˢᵀ TIMOTHY 4:13

Church doctrines are simply the central themes of God's revelation for church practice found in Scripture. This is no exhaustive list. However, we believe these ten articles summarize our interpretation and convictions regarding the local church doctrine.

While the talk of doctrine can seem intimidating and intellectual, these beliefs are not without purpose. Together, these doctrines create a spiritual destination—a local church culture that's built upon the Word of God.

In developing this collection of truths, our objective was to establish an ecclesiology that can be adopted and endorsed by all Reformation Fellowship house churches in all locations across the globe. We believe the Bible's call for local church practice is universal; therefore, it cannot be inhibited by any social disadvantages, privileges, or economics which can differ from culture to culture.

While we believe in the freedom to add extra-curricular, biblically-aligned practices (youth programs, membership classes, worship bands, etc.) to the local church expression, we do not believe these personalized demonstrations can be considered doctrinal or required. In fact, in some cases, they have proven unfruitful.[1] We believe the Bible's prescription for local church practice must be transnational and cross-cultural. It must be possible in a persecuted country as well as a supportive one. It must be possible in the poorest of nations as well as the highest peaks of society. Like the Gospel, any version of church assembly that is not usable and accessible by all cannot be *purely* biblical. That is to say, any version that *requires* a large building or congregational affluence or salaried staff or religious freedom or higher education or civil peace is, in some sense, imposing extra-biblical preferences onto the biblical design for local Christian assembly.

Below, you will find the Reformation Fellowship doctrines for a local house church. We believe they are each wholly supported by Scripture and, together, form a fruitful and holy gathering of believers who glorify God in their local community.

---

1 Scott T. Brown. *A Weed in the Church*, (Raleigh: Merchant Adventurers) 2011.

Church Doctrines
ARTICLES

ARTICLE 01. CHURCH

WE BELIEVE there is one holy Church of Jesus Christ seen in two distinct forms—local and universal (Rom 12:5; 1 Cor. 12:20; 1 Tim. 3:15). The first includes professing believers in Jesus Christ, who assemble in a biblically-ordered congregation at a particular location on a regular basis. The second includes all professing believers in Jesus Christ (past, present, and future) living across the globe.

WE BELIEVE in the autonomy of the local church, free from any external authority or control, with the right of self-government and freedom from the interference of any hierarchy of any outside individuals or organizations (Tit. 1:5). We teach that it is scriptural for true churches to cooperate with each other for the presentation and propagation of the faith. Each local church, however, through its elders and their interpretation and application of Scripture, should be the sole judge of the measure and method of its cooperation. The elders should determine all other matters of membership, policy, discipline, benevolence, and government primarily through Holy Scripture and secondarily through their guiding Confession of Faith (The 1689 L.B.C.F.) (Acts 15:19–31; 20:28; 1 Cor. 5:4–7, 13; 1 Pet. 5:1–4).[1]

ARTICLE 02. MISSION

WE BELIEVE the mission of the Church is: To go into the world and make disciples by declaring the Gospel of Jesus Christ by the power of the Spirit and gathering these disciples into churches, that they might worship and obey Jesus Christ now and in eternity to the glory of God the Father (Matt. 28:16-20).[2] As a result, the church must concentrate its efforts to edify and nourish its members through biblical doctrine, spiritual gifts, and relational duties of love (Eph. 4:11-16; Romans 12:3-21; 1 Cor. 12). Additionally, local churches must not only train members to present the Gospel message to others but also demonstrate the Gospel in their lives—its power, fruitfulness, and hope to an onlooking world (Matt. 5:13-16; 1 Peter 3:15). Through this Great Commission-centric practice of church missiology, we believe the Lord will build His Church (Matt. 16:18) and gather these disciples into local communities (1 Cor. 12:18) where they can worship, obey, and grow in Jesus Christ until the Day of His return. That being said, this doctrinal definition does

---

[1] This *Article on the Church* was originally produced by the elders at Grace Community Church in Sun Valley, CA under John MacArthur. It has been adapted, edited, and reproduced here by Reformation Fellowship.

[2] Kevin DeYoung and Greg Gilbert, *What is the Mission of the Church?*, (Wheaton: Crossway), 2011, 241.

not nullify the significant number of commands in Scripture for Christians individually to display mercy and meet the physical needs of the broken and less fortunate in our world (Prov. 19:17, 22:9; 1 John 3:17; Matt. 5:42).

ARTICLE 03. PEOPLE

We believe the Church of Jesus Christ is not a place but a people—the Body of Christ, of which He is the head (Eph. 1:22–23) and Chief Shepherd (1 Pet. 5:4). Furthermore, we believe the local church is the assembly of God's redeemed and baptized people for the *central* purpose of edification and worship and not for the purpose of evangelism and outreach to unbelievers (2 Cor. 6:14; Eph 4:11-12). That said, we do not believe in forbidding unbelievers from attending a local assembly as the Lord may direct an individual for the purpose of hearing the Gospel through the preaching of the Word of God. (1 Cor. 14:24-25; Rom. 10:17).

ARTICLE 04. EVANGELISM

We believe evangelism is the central *outward* ministry of the local church and its members. It is the walking out of the Great Commission by proclamation of the Gospel of Jesus Christ that leads unto salvation. It is an outreach ministry with the aim and hope to compel, convince, convert, and disciple. We believe this ministry is the responsibility of every Christian and is not to be neglected or outsourced only to the leaders of the local church (Matt. 28:19-20; Mark 16:15; Rom. 10:10-17).

ARTICLE 05. UNITY

We believe Jesus Christ calls His Church to extravagant unity (John 17:20-23). In speaking to the local church, we believe unity is brought forth by a sharing of our common faith in Jesus Christ through the lens of Scripture (1 Cor. 1:10). We believe this spiritual unity is achieved not through human endeavoring but only by the work of the Holy Spirit in the life of individual believers (Eph. 4:3-6; 1 Cor. 12:13). Moreover, we believe the substance of local church unity is generated primarily by the alignment of our doctrinal and theological beliefs, our mutually edifying spiritual gifts, and the fulfillment of the "one-another's" seen in Scripture (1 Cor. 12; Rom. 12:15; Phil. 2:2; Rom. 15:1-5).

It is worth mentioning while unity on doctrines such as The Sufficiency of Scripture, Theology Proper, Christology, Soteriology, Ecclesiology, and the historic evangelical Gospel is imperative, we do not believe that local church unity requires complete doctrinal and theological uniformity. We believe non-teaching, local church members must be provided the latitude in non-essential doctrines, worship style, and personal spiritual demonstration as long as they do not violate the Holy Scriptures. We believe through this freedom of spiritual expression, a diverse assembly of believers can remain supernaturally united under the headship of Christ (1 Cor 12:12). That said, we believe the local church eldership must remain uniform in their doctrine and theology to provide a united presentation of biblical truth (1 Cor. 1:10).

ARTICLE 06. MEETING

WE BELIEVE a church meeting is a formally declared assembly of local church members for the purpose of worship (e.g., the Sunday gathering). We believe the meeting is to be conducted under the doctrines of orderly worship found in 1 Corinthians 11:17-34; 12; 14:26-40, 1 Timothy 2:1-15; 3-4, and Titus 1-3. While there are additional passages that speak to the local church, we believe these central ecclesiastical passages form up a majority of the doctrine regarding local assembly. That is, they beckon for a Spirit-led, elder-governed, contributor-centric, gender role-invoked, edification-focused, and orderly Christian assembly.

In the matter of preaching (*further discussed in Convictions 02-03*), we rely on the language in the *1689 Baptist Confession of Faith*, which states, "Although it be incumbent on the bishops or pastors of the churches to be instant in preaching the word, by way of office, yet the work of preaching the word is not so peculiarly confined to them but that others also gifted and fitted by the Holy Spirit for it, and approved and called by the church, may and ought to perform it."[3] (1 Pet. 4:10-11; 1 Cor. 14:26-33). Additionally, we view the historical, four-part pattern (teaching doctrine, fellowship, breaking bread, and prayer) of the early church assembly seen in Acts 2:42 as a broad yet instructive example for the structure of a local church assembly.

In accordance with Scripture, we encourage all church

---

[3] Stan Reeves. *The 1689 Baptist Confession of Faith in Modern English* (Cape Coral, FL: Founders Press, 2017).

members to be in both prayer and study prior to the assembled meeting with the expectation that the Holy Spirit may lead them, in harmony with their biblical role, at the appropriate time, to share an edifying truth, prayer, short teaching, song of praise, or scriptural illumination during the open meeting of the assembly. We believe the local church is the place where members can both contribute and exercise their spiritual gifts, according to Scripture, under the oversight of qualified elders for the building up of the church (Rom. 12:6-8; 1 Pet. 4:10-11; 1 Cor. 12; Eph. 4:11-16).

Moreover, we believe the Apostle Paul voiced his preference concerning prayer in the local church and that it is to be carried out by the men, "I desire therefore that the men pray everywhere, lifting up holy hands, without wrath and doubting…" (1 Tim. 2:8). That is to say, we believe the weekly church meeting is a venue God has chosen to display His spiritual structure for the family (Eph. 5:22-33; 1 Cor. 11:3; 1 Tim. 2:12-14; Gen. 3:16)

In speaking to gender roles, with regard to a woman's role during local church meetings, we look to the doctrines seen in 1 Corinthians 14:34-35 and 1 Timothy 2:8-12. While we do not believe the text is commanding a complete prohibition of women participating in the church meeting, we do believe the text prohibits women from teaching and assuming spiritual authority during this specific period of time. We do believe, however, the Scriptures permit women during the church gathering, at the appropriate time, to share personal testimonies, offer encouragements, sing, make prayer requests, and deliver church-related announcements. We believe these gender role doctrines are not for the purpose of female oppression but rather God's means to display creation order (1 Cor. 11:8-10), preserve the biblical structure for the family (Eph. 5:22-33), and protect against male spiritual passivity (Gen. 3:6-13.). Having said that, it's important to affirm that we do believe women are equally valuable before God (Gal. 3:28) but different in role within the local church assembly. Likewise, we do not believe women are bound to these ecclesiastical doctrines outside of the local church meeting. In fact, we believe God gifts and equips both men and women as it pertains to teaching, evangelism, and outreach ministry.

In relation to children in the church meeting, we believe Scripture instructs families to worship together. Otherwise stated, we do not believe the Bible encourages children's church or Sunday School. We believe the responsibility of child discipleship is to be carried out by parents (Deut. 6:6-7; Eph. 6:4; Prov. 22:6; Col 3:20-21). That said, children (excluding babies) over time will learn (with patience from the adults—and maybe a few toys) to sit quietly and observe others and their parents during the church assembly.

ARTICLE 07. WORSHIP

WE BELIEVE God's people are a singing people (Col. 3:16; Ps. 100:1-2). However, what the modern church has identified as *worship*, the Bible has identified as *songs of praise* (Ps. 68:4; Ps. 69:30; Ps 95:1-11; Ps. 147:1;). In that regard, corporate musical praise is a form of worship and for that reason, should conform to the biblical instruction for such activity.

In John 4:24-25 it states, "But the hour is coming, and now is, when the true worshipers will worship the Father in *spirit and truth*; for the Father is seeking such to worship Him. God is Spirit, and those who worship Him must worship in spirit and truth" (italics added for emphasis). This principle of fastening heart-centered worship to biblical-centered truth speaks thunderously that the worship of God, whether by prayer or by preaching or by singing, must be done reverently and in alignment with the Word of God.

As it pertains to principles of worship, there are two schools of thought. The first is called the *normative principle of worship* and states that a congregation can do anything not forbidden in Scripture. That said, this perspective offers an open door to a wide variety of church and worship expressions that, throughout church history, has proven unfruitful and even dangerous. We believe it is not enough to simply *not do* what is forbidden by Scripture; we believe we *must do* only what is commanded in Scripture. For that reason, we adopt the alternative—the *regulative principle of worship*. That is, we believe a congregation may only do that which is commanded in Scripture. It is from this place that we worship God as He commanded not as we desire (Gen. 4:3–8; Exod. 25:40; Deut. 12:4; 1 Sam. 15:22; Matt. 15:1–14; Col. 2:18;).

Furthermore, we believe a congregation learns their theology not only by the preaching they hear or by the prayers they pray but also by the songs they sing. For that reason, we believe songs of praise must hold to the same theological and doctrinal accuracy that is expected of a preacher's sermon

(Jam. 3:1; 1 Pet. 4:11). The Apostle Paul furthers this idea of truth-bound and comprehensible praise and worship in 1 Corinthians 14:15 where he states, "I will pray with the spirit, and I will also pray with the understanding. I will sing with the spirit, and I will also sing with the understanding." In summation, we do not believe in accommodating worship music that takes such creative license that it causes theological confusion or misunderstanding.

Lastly, we believe a congregation's behavior during worship is to be orderly and exhibiting the fruits of the Spirit, including self-control (1 Cor. 14:33; Gal. 5:22-23; 2 Tim. 1:7). Now, that does not mean that members cannot express their devotion to God through passionate praise or the raising of hands and voices, but it does mean that we do so in a way that maintains harmony with the congregation and reverence before God.

ARTICLE 08. GOVERNANCE

WE BELIEVE only two offices constitute biblical church government: Elders and Deacons. These are two separate offices with separate responsibilities. To put it briefly, elders fulfill the spiritual shepherding duties while deacons attend to the physical needs of the flock. Below is a brief overview of both offices and how they relate to the congregation.

Elder: In the New Testament, we see a variety of words used to describe this office—"elder" (*presbuteros*), "overseer" (*episkopos*), and "pastor" (*poimēn*). While the modern church most commonly uses the latter term (pastor) to identify this position, we will learn that Scripture uses all three of these terms to describe this one office. To support this doctrinal perspective, 1 Timothy 3:1-7 presents the qualifications for an overseer (*episkopos*) which are nearly identical to the qualifications for an elder (*presbuteros*) in Titus 1:6-9. In fact, in the passage seen in Titus 1, Paul uses both of these terms in reference to the same office (*presbuteros* in v. 5 and *episkopos* in v. 7). Additionally, in both Acts 20 and 1 Peter 5:1-2, we see all three of these words used interchangeably throughout the text. In short, these three words used in Scripture are not to identify three different offices but to showcase the variety of ministerial duties involved within the singular office of Elder.[4]

Qualifications and Responsibilities: To preface, Jesus Christ is the ultimate Shepherd of His Church. However, in Scripture, He has commissioned and appointed under-shepherds (elders) to guide, feed, and protect His local flocks (Acts 20:28). For this reason, 1 Timothy 3:2-7 and Titus 1:6-8 demand the highest requirements of character for the men who are called to this spiritual office. As a central qualification, elders are to be above reproach. They are to be married men with children. As 1 Timothy 3:5 clearly states, "For if a man does not know how to rule his own house, how will he take care of the church of God?"

In terms of spiritual responsibilities, their chief duties are to both preach sound doctrine and protect against false

---

[4] John Piper. *Biblical Eldership*. DesiringGod.org, accessed March 16, 2020, www.desiringgod.org/messages/biblical-eldership-session-1.

doctrine. As a result, the office of Elder is the highest level of local church leadership and carries the greatest amount of spiritual responsibility (Heb. 13:17; Jam. 3:1).

As a caretaker of the local church, these overseers of the flock are to determine church policy (Acts 15:22); oversee the church (Acts 20:28); appoint others for church government (Titus 1:5); rule, teach, and preach (1 Tim. 5:17; cf. 1 Thess. 5:12; 1 Tim. 3:2). They are to exhort and refute (Titus 1:9). But at the heart, they are to act as shepherds, directing and setting an example for all (1 Pet. 5:1-3).[5]

In relation to the congregation, Scripture calls for the members of a local church to recognize and esteem (1 Thess. 5:12-13), spiritually submit and emulate (Heb. 13:7; Heb. 13:17; 1 Pet. 5:5-6), grant honor, and financially support (1 Tim. 5:17-18), and to not receive an accusation against them without the presence of two or three witnesses (1 Tim. 5:19-20). Furthermore, the congregation is to hold these individuals to the strict standards of Scripture while also extending grace and understanding in times of repentant error. While these men serve a vital role in the local church, it is important to state that their authority is spiritual and not physical. These men are to be revered and respected, but they are not to be viewed as possessing control of any particular church member's personal decisions, relationships, family, or resources.

Deacon: The Greek word *diakonos* is translated to "deacon"

---

[5] John MacArthur. *The Master's Plan for the Church* (Chicago: Moody Press, 1991).

in the English language and means "servant" or "minister" (Rom. 15:8; 1 Cor. 3:5; Cor. 3:6; Col 1:23). This word is used in a variety of passages in Scripture to reference servanthood or acts of church service (Matt. 20:26; Acts 11:29; 12:25; 19:22; Rom. 15:31; 2 Cor. 8:4; 9:1, 12, 13). Having said that, this is not an examination of its verb presentation but its noun format (1 Tim. 8-13; Eph. 6:21; 1 Thess. 3:2;). That is, there is a Christian duty of service, and then there is the office of formalized Church Servant. Deacons do not replace the scriptural requirement of church members to serve one another. However, they are a great additional benefit to local church leadership and should be honored and respected for their humble service.

Qualifications and Responsibilities: The qualifications for these commissioned servants can be found in 1 Timothy 3:8-13. Unlike the office of elder, the deacon's responsibilities are limited to local church servanthood and not to interfere with congregational shepherding. In essence, the deacons are authorized individuals utilized by the elder(s) to accommodate and organize meeting the physical needs of the local congregation. This may include spiritual encouragement, informational meetings, hospitality, baptism, the facilitation of the Lord's Supper, financial burdens, lodging, personal sustenance, health requirements, and emergencies. Biblically speaking, it is the deacons who help diversify the physical demands of the flock from the elder(s) to ensure their efforts of spiritual leadership, study, and preaching can remain uninterrupted (Acts 6:1-4).

We believe, according to Scripture, that formalized and appointed deacons are to be married men with children. 1 Timothy 3:11-12 states, "Likewise, their [deacon's] wives must be reverent, not slanderers, temperate, faithful in all things. Let deacons be the husbands of one wife, ruling their children and their own houses well." As previously stated, we believe all Christians are called to serve the church; however, the Scriptures make an indicated difference between a Christian's common service and the office of Deacon. In 1 Timothy 3:10 the text states, "But let these also first be tested; then let them serve as deacons, being found blameless." This testing and examination prior to service imply a clear distinction between the universal service all Christians are called to perform and the special service to be carried out by proven (tested) and appointed Deacons. While some have used the argument of Phoebe in Romans 16:1 who is referenced as a deacon in the local church to justify female Deacons, we believe, since the word *diakonos* (which is used 29 times in the New Testament) simply means *servant*, Paul used this term as a description of her fervent Christian service to the local church and not as an identifying term of her formalized church office.

ARTICLE 09. DISCIPLINE

We believe church discipline is God's mode of purification for His church and His method for the protection of His reputation in the world. In fact, history confirms discipline must be exercised in the Church, for, without it, it would soon look like the culture. We believe any person who identifies themselves as a Christian is to be held to the spiritual and moral standards of that public profession set forth in the Scriptures (Rom. 16:17-18; 2 Thess. 3:13-15; 2 John 1:9-10). The letter of 1 Corinthians clearly supports this belief when it states, "But now I am writing to you not to associate with anyone who bears the name of brother if he is guilty of sexual immorality or greed, or is an idolater, reviler, drunkard, or swindler—not even to eat with such a one." (5:11). This passage goes on to say, "For what have I to do with judging outsiders? Is it not those inside the church whom you are to judge? God judges those outside. 'Purge the evil person from among you.'" (5:12-13). In short, Christians are not to tolerate brothers or sisters walking in known, unrepentant sin. As a matter of fact, we are not even to associate with these individuals unless it is for the explicit purpose of exhortation (Gal. 6:1; 2 Thess. 3:13-15). In the Gospels, The Lord Himself furthers the demand for church discipline by giving His people a very specific process for dealing with those in the local church who are caught in personal or public sin.

In Matthew 18:15-17, He says, "If your brother sins against you, go and tell him his fault, between you and him alone. If he listens to you, you have gained your brother. But if he does not listen, take one or two others along with you, that every charge may be established by the evidence of two or three witnesses. If he refuses to listen to them, tell it to the church. And if he refuses to listen even to the church, let him be to you as a Gentile and a tax collector."

The Lord's grace continues to shine forth as we see His model uphold an obvious progression from gentle private correction to harsh public excommunication. Regardless of the stage of discipline and correction, our deepest hope, as Christians, should always be for full restoration (2 Cor. 2:5-11; Jam. 5:19-20). Additionally, it is never to be a joy to inflict correction or church discipline but a duty as a brother or sister in Christ (1 Cor. 5:2). Nonetheless, it is worth stating that in the case of a personal offense, the Scriptures do teach that it is both to our glory to overlook a personal transgression (Prov. 19:11) and to our dignity to allow our love for another Christian to cover a multitude of sins (1 Pet. 4:8). That being said, we believe it is not loving to overlook a pattern of sin or dangerous moral failure that is damaging to the wrongdoer, others, or to the reputation of Christ and His Church.

We believe correction in connection to personal offense is a shared duty of all church members. However, we believe more advanced or severe cases of church discipline fall upon the congregation under the guidance of the elders who are "to give an account" of the spiritual status of the flock to Christ (Heb. 13:17).

Lastly, we believe correction and church discipline are vital parts of a biblical church, and, as people who sin, every church member should expect to experience a moment of correction as long as they are in a scripturally-guided community with other believers. According to Scripture, this experience of correction should produce humility, repentance, restoration, and gratitude (Prov. 9:8; Prov. 11:2; Prov. 12:15; Luke 17:3-4; Heb. 12:11; Jam. 4:6). In fact, the Bible says that only a fool despises correction (Prov. 1:7; Prov. 27:5-6).

In closing, church discipline is to be viewed as a blessing. To have a community of people acting as guard rails and protecting one's spiritual health, the state of their family, and their status within the church is a tremendous benefit to the Christian life.

ARTICLE 10. GIVING

We believe church members are strongly encouraged by Scripture to financially participate in three forms of giving. **(1)** Giving to the elders who fulfill spiritual labors for the benefit of the local congregation (1 Cor. 9:5-12; Luke 10:7; 1 Tim. 5:18; Gal. 6:6, Jam. 5:4-5). **(2)** Giving to the local and global needs of the saints (1 John 3:17; Heb. 13:16; Rom. 12:13; Jam. 2:15-16; Gal. 6:2; 1 Cor. 16:1-4). **(3)** Giving to the poor (Prov. 19:17; Prov. 22:9; Matt. 5:42; Luke 12:33; Matt. 25:35-45; Matt. 19:21; Mark 12:41-44;). Additionally, we believe the New Testament's call for generosity has superseded the Old Testament's call for tithing. We, as New Covenant Christians, are not under the jurisdiction of the Old Covenant (Eph. 2:15; Gal. 2:19) and, as a result, are relieved from the command of tithing to the Levite priesthood and to the ministerial needs of the temple. Instead, we are commanded to be generous with one another under the law of love (2 Corinthians 9:6-8). We do believe giving, in any format, is a private matter only to be known by those who give and receive and by the Lord (Matt. 6:3-4). While we do not believe an unwillingness to give is grounds for church discipline, we do believe Christians who refuse to contribute to the ministry and shepherds in which they directly benefit have an incorrect and immature spiritual posture that should be brought before the Lord in prayer.

In a biblical house church, giving to the ministry and its shepherds can vary. Additionally, a giver should not expect a tax benefit for their gift as churches in Reformation Fellowship are not government-sanctioned organizations, nor are they tax-exempt. That said, gifts between individuals may have unique tax opportunities. Look into your local and federal tax laws for further financial guidance.

In general, Reformation Fellowship pastors should make it clear to church members regarding a preferred process for giving. For some churches, it might be an offering box in the home; for others, it may be accomplished electronically or by check or cash in person. Regardless of the elected financial vehicle, giving pathways should be made clear by the pastor but pursued by the individual church member.

As for giving to others in the local church, it is the responsibility of the members to present their needs publicly or privately so they may be met by other members.

SECTION 04: CONVICTIONS

"Absolutes define the core beliefs of the Christian faith; convictions, while not core beliefs, do have significant impact on the health and effectiveness of the church..."

Erik Thoennes

Introduction
CHURCH CONVICTIONS

"The faith which you have, have as your own conviction before God. Happy is he who does not condemn himself in what he approves."

ROMANS 14:22

It was Martin Luther who said, "For to go against conscience is neither right nor safe."[1] Different from the previous section on Church Doctrine, Church Convictions are matters of organizational conscience and scriptural interpretation. While many, if not most historic Christian churches would align with these perspectives, these are positions based on biblical principles, not specific commands of Scripture.

However, these convictions have not simply been helpful to our network of house churches; they have also been fruitful. Within these convictions are much of the makings of the rich biblical culture Reformation Fellowship champions. Additionally, we, as a network of church planters and pastors, have borne witness to the positive evidence that has resulted

---

[1] Roland H. Bainton. *Here I Stand; A life of Martin Luther.* (New York: Mentor, 1950).

from their application in the local house church setting.

Reformation Fellowship Convictions
ARTICLES

ARTICLE 01. APPOINTMENT

While an exact sequence is not directly organized in Scripture, we believe the New Testament displays a clear set of five chronological events for the appointment of elders and deacons in the local church.

1. Gifting: A man has an evident spiritual gift for teaching, pastoral care, and servanthood (1 Cor. 12:7-11; 1 Tim 3:1; Eph. 4:11).

2. Qualifying: A man meets the biblical qualifications for the office of Elder or Deacon (1 Tim. 3:1-13; Tit. 1:5-9).

3. Anointing: A man, through personal conviction and demonstration of that conviction within the congregation, is called by God to the office (Acts 20:28; Eph. 4:11-12).

4. Recognizing: A man, through congregational recognition and validation, is selected to fill the office (Acts 6:3).

5. Appointing: A man, by the power of either existing elders and local church leaders or an established ecclesiastical body (e.g. Reformation Fellowship), is to be appointed to the office by the laying on of hands (Acts 14:23; Tit. 1:5).

In an effort to maintain ecclesiological purity and unity, elders and deacons of local assemblies who desire to be formally included in Reformation Fellowship are required to substantially affirm both the 1689 L.B.C.F and Doctrines and Convictions found within this handbook.

ARTICLE 02. EXPOSITORY PREACHING

We believe it should be the aim of those shepherding or teaching in the local church to centralize and prioritize expository teaching over topical teaching. That is, any sermon or teaching should find its sole source of the content in Scripture, and the substance of the teaching should be retrieved through careful exegesis and proper hermeneutics.[1] Furthermore, expositors seek to align the interpretation of the biblical text within the larger doctrinal truths seen throughout Scripture. Moreover, teachers will always connect their sermons to the Bible's greater narrative and present how Christ, the final fulfillment of the text, is the central focus of all Scripture.

---

1 John MacArthur. *Preaching: How to Preach Biblically* (Nashville: Thomas Nelson, 2005).

We also believe that a church who is convicted to proclaim all of Scripture will never allow any significant portion of the Bible to be ignored.[2] In Acts 20:27, Paul declares, "for I did not shrink from declaring to you the whole counsel of God." For this reason, we believe it is right for shepherds and teachers to direct their preaching efforts in a systematic, verse-by-verse format that does not avoid certain passages of Scripture due to unpopularity, lack of cultural comfort, or complexity.

Because God's Word is what converts, convicts, edifies, corrects, and sanctifies those in the Church (Heb. 4:12; Rom. 10:17; 1 Pet. 1:23; 1 Thess. 2:13; John. 17:17), elders, preachers, and teachers must make Scripture the center of the sermon. In short, the goal of the expository preacher is not to hear, "What a great sermon" or "What an uplifting message" but to hear from their church members, "Thank you, I now understand what that biblical passage means and how it applies to my life."

ARTICLE 03. BIBLICAL THEOLOGY

We believe both elders and church members should have a firm understanding of biblical theology. That is, we believe the strength and health of a local church are dependent upon its individual members comprehending the arrangement and agreement of the Scriptures as one unified story (1 Tim. 1:5, 2 John 1-6, and Titus 2:1-10). When a church establishes a doctrinal culture of biblical theology, members will prevent

---

[2] Bryan Chapel. *Christ-Centered Preaching: Redeeming the Expository Sermon* (Ada Michigan: Baker Academic, 2005).

any individual portions of Scripture from being extracted and interpreted from the whole. Instead, both preachers and members will recognize that all Scripture, while organized in covenants and books and chapters, is one consistent and historically revealed plan of redemption culminating in the birth, ministry, death, resurrection, and ascension of Jesus Christ.

ARTICLE 04. HOUSES

While a biblical church meeting can theoretically take place anywhere (a garage, under a tree, in a building, etc.), we are convicted that the house offers the most effective setting to generate the intimacy, closeness, and security required to walk out the level of love seen between church members in the New Testament. Some argue that the New Testament Christians only met in homes because they could not gather elsewhere. While this might hold some truth in a pragmatic sense, we do not believe that having access to public buildings today should decrease the biblical example and benefits of house gatherings found in the Scriptures (Acts 2:46; Acts 5:42; 20:20 ; 1 Cor. 16:19; Rom. 16:5; Col. 4:15; Phil. 1:2).

Furthermore, and most beneficially, meeting in homes forces groups to be small and deeply connected while also encouraging the sense of family that seems to be missing between most Christians today. Lastly, and more practically speaking, house gatherings alleviate the legalities of incorporation, reduce the risk of persecution (for those living in hostile areas), and eliminate the massive financial weight of a church building and its operations. In short, because church members already have homes available to them, the money allocated for a traditional church venue can be reinvested into supporting their pastor and meeting other spiritual needs.

We believe it is beneficial but not mandatory for house churches to rotate homes at some predetermined frequency (e.g., every eight weeks). Ideally, the act of hosting and serving the local church should be a shared activity not to be absorbed strictly by the elders or by one or two families. However, because hosting is an indirect form of church influence, we believe it should not be carried out by those young in their faith or new to a particular assembly. Additionally, each local church will be limited by the geography, parking, liabilities, and square footage of the homes within its membership.

> **Suggestion:** In connection to homes, we have found it beneficial but not necessary for churches to create a church-hosting kit complete with folding chairs, pulpit, hymnals, songbooks, and dishware. Some gatherings have even included a guitar, high chairs, communion set, and extra Bibles.

ARTICLE 05. FELLOWSHIP

The word *fellowship* is a term that has been vandalized by the Western Church. In other words, we have distorted it into an expression that has lost much of its original meaning. The Greek word for fellowship is *koinonia [koi·no·nia]*, and it does not merely signify Christian friendship or even Christian gathering. Biblically speaking, *koinonia* is displayed as an interactive, reciprocating, and participating relationship with both God and others believers who share in their mutual new-life through Christ (Acts 2:42; 1 John 1:3, 6–7; 2 Cor. 9:13; Phil. 3:10).

That is to say, to experience biblical fellowship is to engage in the sharing of both spiritual giving and spiritual receiving. It is the spiritual ethic that while we may have no secular attributes in common (where we live, what we enjoy, our ethnicity, our age, etc.), we can still find and experience rich exchanging of fellowship through our joint faith in Jesus Christ.

Furthermore, we believe true fellowship is anchored in intentional relationship. Namely, biblical fellowship cannot take root in a local church that nurtures "audience Christianity" or "spectator Christianity." The Bible is clear that church members are to purpose themselves to contribute and reciprocate with one another in love. It is through this self-denying, one-anothering, servanthood-centered culture that we can eradicate the all-too-common spirit of independence that plagues many of today's churches. For this reason, we believe local churches should strive to cultivate fellowship by allowing for time not only during the Sunday assembly but also throughout the week. We believe that genuine fellowship must integrate daily by weaving itself into a rich communal culture on mission for the Gospel.

Suggestion: We have found it fruitful but not mandatory for local churches to host 90-min, mid-week, fellowship-focused men's gatherings and women's gatherings. This layer of intentional fellowship time greatly strengthens the bond between believers and allows for a more united meeting on Sunday.

ARTICLE 06. DISCIPLESHIP

As part of the Great Commission (Matt. 28:18-20), Christians are to make disciples. This does not mean we are called to make converts, for only God can convert a sinner to a saint. This also does not mean we are to produce disciples in *our way* of Christianity. Rather, we are commanded to produce and strengthen disciples of Christ through the preaching and hearing of God's Word (Rom. 10:17) and through Christian fellowship, encouragement, accountability, correction, and intercessory prayer (Hebrews 10:24-25).

In the local church setting, while we believe the elders are primarily responsible for church-wide discipleship through expository preaching, we also believe one-on-one discipleship in its many forms (teaching, guiding, praying, correcting, exhorting, encouraging, etc.) is the duty of every Christian. That said, while the Scriptures call men to lead the church as a whole, we, by a complementarian conviction and alignment with the *Danvers Statement of Biblical Manhood and Womanhood,* maintain that women are called to lead the women and men are called to lead men in their interpersonal relationships.[3]

Furthermore, we believe this one-on-one discipleship

---

3 The Council on Biblical Manhood and Womanhood. *Danvers Statement.* Danvers, Massachusetts, December 1988, cbmw.org/about/danvers-statement/.

is to be ordered according to spiritual maturity, age, and biblical role. For example, Titus 2:1-10 commands proper examples of older men to be displayed for the younger men and for older women to teach younger women how to love their husbands and their children.

Lastly, we believe parents are to be the leading source of discipleship for their children, but they are not to be the only source. In our judgment, the warning of Matthew 18:6 is to be seriously considered in any discipleship activity but especially in the discipleship of a young believer, "But whoever causes one of these little ones who believe in me to sin, it would be better for him to have a great millstone fastened around his neck and to be drowned in the depth of the sea." Discipleship in the local church is a weighty and consequential assignment in which all Christians are to engage with a pure heart and a yielded spirit to God's Word.

ARTICLE 07. OUTREACH

God, through the Great Commission (Matt. 28:18-20), has called the members of His Church to the work of evangelism and outreach. However, we believe the term "outreach" more accurately describes the pragmatic nature of this crucial ministry—which is outward. That is, we believe evangelism is intended to an external ministry of the local church and not internal. We, as members of a local church, are called to share the verbal Gospel (Rom. 10:17; Matt. 28:18-20) through all means available to us as an assembly of God's people.

Nevertheless, we do not believe Christians should invite their unsaved friends to the local church meeting as a way to offload their spiritual responsibility of Gospel sharing to their pastor or others within their church community. According to Scripture, evangelism is the work of every Christian (2 Cor. 5:18-20; Matt. 5:14-16; 1 Pet. 3:15; Phil. 2:14-16; Col. 4:5-6; 1 Pet. 2:9). We, as individual believers, are to pray the Lord grants us each opportunities both publicly and in our private relationships to share His Gospel faithfully. In the event we experience a person who displays the genuine fruits of conversion by our preaching, we believe Christians are to follow the biblical example of inviting that individual to gather with the people of God in the local church, baptizing that individual in the presence of God's people, and teaching that individual the commandments of God's Word. (Matt. 28:18-20).

Having said that, we do not believe in human-led Gospel promotion. Throughout the Scriptures, those who preached publicly were led by the Spirit, and those who preached privately were led by the Spirit (1 Thess. 1:5; 1 Pet. 1:12; Acts 4:8-12; 6:10 13:4-5; 16:6; 1 Cor. 2:4-5; 2:13; John 14:26). We are not to turn God's mission of evangelism into man's efforts of soul-saving. We believe the Lord calls each of us to be prepared, ready, and willing to share the Good News with others (2 Tim. 4:2, 1 Pet. 3:15; 2 Cor. 5:17-19). With this biblical perspective, we can trust that God's ministry will never compromise His other commands regarding marriage, family, friendships, finances, and church. God, whose will is perfect, will remove any obstacles and prepare all paths for His message to be heard.

Suggestion: We have found it incredibly fruitful but not mandatory for local church members to commit to weekly or monthly outreach in their own hometown. Namely, to preach the Gospel in the open air, have one-on-one conversations with neighbors, and hand out Gospel tracts and Bibles to the public. To have a local church who claims the Gospel is their central mission yet never forms an organized effort to carry out that mission in their own neighborhood is puzzling. *Note: Our companion ministry at MailtheGospel.org offers Gospel tracts to Reformation Fellowship members at a discounted rate.*

ARTICLE 08. GUESTS

One might wonder why a process for inviting guests to a church gathering is so important that it demanded an entire article in this document? If you share in this curiosity, it is likely a result of your westernized perspective of the local church. For those planting, leading, and attending underground house churches in persecuted countries, however, invitation, and the process of it is critical. Church members should know not only the biblical parameters of church invitation but also the scriptural wisdom that can uphold order, physical safety, and the spiritual health for those already in the local flock.

Due to the nature of an every-member-functioning gathering, it's important to recognize that any member is permitted to invite guests, and any invited guest is biblically permitted to participate in the meeting in some way or another. Additionally, these guests will also be brought into the presence of the church's children and the personal home and life of the church member hosting at that particular time. For this reason, we believe it is very important to first determine that visitors are truly born-again believers and not false converts, heretics, persecutors, or wolves in sheep's clothing.

We will separate our suggested process of invitation into three groups:

Non-believers: The local church, the Body of Christ, is first and foremost an assembly of believers for the edification of believers. Nonetheless, we are not to prohibit the lost from attending the local church meeting (1 Cor. 14:24-25). However, the allowing of non-believers in the local assembly and a church culture that encourages members to invite non-believers is very different. As stated in our conviction regarding outreach—evangelism is presented scripturally as an outward ministry of the local church. That is to say, we believe inviting non-believers to the local church meeting is to put things in the wrong order. Scripture generally demonstrates that conversion precedes visitation in the local church. Now, if a non-believer shows up to a local church meeting, we are to embrace this person and allow them to hear the Gospel and see the power of God in the presence of His people (1 Cor. 14:24-25).

As it pertains to the invitation of professed, born-again, and baptized Christians, we believe it's useful to break these guests into two groups: Non-Local Christian Visitors and Local Christians Who Are Potential Members.

Non-Local Christian Visitors: All church members at some point will be presented with Christian friends or family who have found themselves in town during your Sunday church gathering. If these Christian friends have an interest in attending your house church, Reformation Fellowship encourages you to bring them. However, our experience has taught us that many Christians have never experienced a biblical house church assembly and may be uncomfortable with church doctrine regarding gender roles or children being present or even certain sermon content. For that reason, we suggest setting theological, doctrinal, and structural expectations with your guests prior to the church meeting. We also recommend notifying the members of your church as a courtesy as it does change the intimacy of the assembly.

Local Christians Who Are Potential Members: 1 Corinthians 12:18 boldly states, "But now God has set the members, each one of them, in the body just as He pleased." That is to say, we do not need to convince or compel any individual or family to join our specific church. In fact, we should allow their decision to be purely driven by the Lord's leading. In Matthew 16:18 Jesus says, "I will build My church, and the gates of Hades shall not prevail against it." In other words, it is not us who build, and, for that reason, we can rest. It is simply the church member's duty to be faithful to the Scriptures, hospitable to every guest, and be prepared to offer answers to any practical questions visitors may ask. In terms of the visitation process for the specific possibility of becoming members of the church, the following steps, which are strictly suggestive, have proven fruitful for our network churches:

1. The most organic first step is to invite the interested individual or family over for dinner as a way of personal introduction (this typically occurs naturally). During your time, ask to hear their Christian testimony, find out if they have been baptized, inquire why they are searching for a new local church (be sure there is no conflict at their previous church that needs to be resolved first), discuss their view and posture toward the Bible, learn about their theological and doctrinal positions, and see if they have any questions about your specific gathering.

2. As a way to present clear definitions and unambiguous expectations, consider giving the individual or family a copy of this handbook. You can also send them to ReformationFellowship.org. However, we have found that guests are generally grateful to have a printed resource that answers their deeper theological and ecclesiastical questions. Next, ask them to review the website and/or handbook and bring any questions or concerns to a follow-up dinner, coffee, or meet-up.

3. After the individual or family has had their questions answered and if they have determined they are in alignment with the doctrines, convictions, and liturgical structure of Reformation Fellowship, extend an invitation to attend the Sunday assembly and any fellowship gatherings for the next several weeks (4-8 weeks is typical in our experience).

4. After this multi-week window of visitation, prayer, and engagement with the other church members, request the individual or family to make a public announcement regarding their decision to either join or move on to another church. If the Lord leads them to join your church, one of the elders should set up a meeting to have them review and complete the Reformation Fellowship Membership Covenant (a short, non-legally-binding document reviewing the expectations for formal church membership).

In closing, making a commitment to a local church is no small decision. We, as church members, are to come alongside visitors in prayer, hospitality, and biblical counsel to assist them in determining the Lord's placement in His Church.

ARTICLE 09. MULTIPLICATION

We believe that widespread multiplication always begins with local devotion. That is to say, expansion of the local church is not built on strategy or salesmanship, or striving. Multiplication is simply the result of persistent faithfulness—faithfulness in preaching God's Word, faithfulness in discipling God's people, and faithfulness in local outreach. It is from this place of internal spiritual investment which God has declared to open the fountain of outgrowth.

Nonetheless, this truth does not eliminate our call to pray

and plan for growth. Men who show the marks of future shepherds, teachers, and servants should be intentionally discipled and theologically trained (Pastors often send these men through our one-year training program at Reformation Seminary (2 Tim. 2:2; 2 Tim. 2:15). Families who are being appointed and sent off into local church ministry should be prayed over, strengthened in encouragement, and prepared for the realities of ministry.

But as one might expect, multiplication (as a functional reality) is generally driven by church size. Now, there is no correct size for a local house church—the Bible does not offer us these specifics. However, biblical example, church history, and even basic sociology indicate that communities thrive when they are small. In our experience, the most fruitful churches typically include 8-12 families and some singles (about 30-50 people, including children). Coincidentally, these numbers also align with the typical space available in the average house (trust us, you can make it work).

In addition to size, the central relational indicator for church multiplication is felt in the loss of the members' ability to maintain deep intimacy and fulfill the "one-another's" commanded in Scripture. This inability to connect deeply with each person (which is generally sensed by the members) is a spiritual signal that, in God's timing, this one gathering should multiply into two.

Multiplication, however, can be very difficult as it does place physical distance and spiritual transition between brothers and sisters who are very close. Nevertheless, we must remember that multiplication is God's work. Therefore, it is good. We, as the Church of God, are not to become stagnant reservoirs but flowing rivers on mission to saturate the culture with the Gospel of Jesus Christ.

Parish-Model Multiplication

One of the strengths of the traditional church model is the capability, diversity, and accountability offered through congregational size. However, we believe the house church can experience these same benefits through what Reformation Fellowship calls "Parishes." When a house church multiplies, the new church plant becomes the second congregation within a parish. There can be up to three house churches in one parish, and there can be an unlimited number of parishes in any given city. Under this multiplication format, individual house churches can stay connected and thereby find greater diversity, capability, and accountability within their parish. That is, while each congregation is independent with its own elders, deacons, and membership, it is locally associated with the other house churches in their parish. This structure permits not only parish-wide events (men and women's retreats, parenting classes, outreach efforts, etc.) but also a larger pool for local church fellowship and elder accountability.

ARTICLE 10. PLANTING

As stated in the previous article, numerical size, along with relational overstrain, are the physical foreshadows of a new house church plant. For those men who both meet the qualifications and are appointed into pastoral ministry, this opportunity will initiate the church planting process.

While Scripture is not specific on the exact process for church planting, the Bible presents a variety of principles that have proven helpful. First, because the initial act of church planting requires shepherding, we are convicted that church planters must be gifted, qualified, anointed, recognized, and appointed elders (See *Doctrine: Article 08 and Conviction: Article 01*).

Second, both Scripture and history have shown that both a plurality of elders and families are essential to a fruitful church plant (1 Cor. 12:1-11; Ecc. 4:12). That is to say, in an ideal situation, we believe a church plant should include at least 1-2 elders and 3-5 families who are stable in doctrinal truth and seasoned in biblical culture. As stated above, plurality without variety is often limiting. For this reason, we believe it's also useful to send off a diversified group of individuals who vary in age, maturity, stage of life, and personality type. While this is not always possible, we believe this multiform effort offers the most fertile soil for fruitful and spiritually safe church establishment.

Finally, we cannot overlook the strenuous and weighty spiritual work of house church planting. In the weeks prior to multiplication and send-off, church members should be in persistent and continual prayer for the new church plant. Furthermore, current elders should be intentional in preparing church planters for the theological and practical duties of pastoral ministry. But most of all, the church must view this new plant as an independently governed but deeply bonded and unified sister church of Jesus Christ (Romans

15:26; 1 Cor. 16:1; Col. 4:7-8; Phil 4:10-23). More specifically, sending church members are to continue to commit themselves to prayer and make themselves available to the individuals and families of the new church plant while it takes root.

Church planting is true missional work. When done under the banner of the Gospel, it is the central way of expanding the visible Kingdom of God on earth. It is an old Hebrew proverb that states, "Apples are not the central fruit of the tree. No… it is new apple trees." It is from this perspective and Commission of God that we labor. To Him be the glory! Amen.

SECTION 05: ORDER OF WORSHIP

"Worship is no longer worship when it reflects the culture around us more than the Christ within us."

A. W. Tozer

Introduction

A FREE-WORSHIP LITURGY

"Let all things be done decently and in order."
1 Corinthians 14:40

Liturgy is simply a term to describe the order in which assembled church worship is conducted. In fact, every local church has some form of liturgy. In the Western evangelical church, it may look something like this:

MODERN CHURCH SERVICE
Welcome > Worship Songs > Prayer > Announcements > Sermon > Altar Call > Offering > Prayer > Dismissal.

In the Presbyterian, Lutheran, or Anglican church, the liturgy is far more robust, including a variety of prayers, recitations, call-and-response activities, Scripture readings, the Lord's Supper, and benediction. Historically speaking, the liturgical templates are endless. Unfortunately, most liturgically focused churches have manufactured extra-biblical, dense, and oftentimes, soul-numbing rituals. Clergy or church overseers from these traditions often overextend their theological aspirations for the flock and bury the biblical objective of assembled worship and edification under a mountain of lifeless activity. Furthermore, by elevating the liturgy beyond the biblical instruction, these churches have squeezed the Holy Spirit's leadership right out of the assembly. That is, through a prioritized dedication to a ceremonial formality, they have replaced the biblical order of worship, the organic leadership of the Spirit, and the congregation's opportunity to participate with the predictable and systematic directorship of man.

On the other hand, the modern church has reduced and watered down the Sunday order of worship to feel more like a cultural event, conference, or concert than a reverent and biblically-directed gathering of God's people. In many churches, it has become a monologue instead of a dialogue, it has become visitor-centric instead of committed-centric, it has become evangelistically focused instead of discipleship focused, it has prioritized theatrics instead of theology, it has become passive instead of active, it has become audience Christianity and not contributor Christianity. That is to say, in a very real sense, the vast majority of churches have either fallen to a hyper-structured and ritualistic liturgy or a hyper-structured and entertaining liturgy.

We believe the Bible has provided an alternative to these two fractured approaches. That is, we believe the Bible offers a local church liturgy that not only calls for orderly praise, prayer, and preaching but also permits space for the directing and prompting of the Holy Spirit, the exercising of spiritual gifts within the body and the mutual edification of the brethren. We have titled this structure a *Free-Worship Liturgy* because it contrasts the painfully predictable and restrictive liturgies previously discussed.

A Free-Worship Liturgy, while still adhering to a pre-planned and structured liturgical outline, offers space between each portion of the meeting for biblically aligned and Spirit-prompted discussion and contribution among the congregation. That is, instead of an assembly ruled solely by calculated order, there becomes room for reverent and edifying engagement that follows the pattern of Scripture.

As you will see, this liturgy follows the Regulative Principle of Worship and finds its sole source in Scripture. That is, every portion of this liturgy is directly demonstrated in Scripture. However, we do acknowledge that not all liturgical elements such as Welcome Statements and Church Announcements can be found in Scripture. That is to say, we believe each house church is permitted to add common sense operational elements to their liturgy based on their unique circumstances. Be that as it may, we also affirm that elders ought to be prudent and slow to add in any extra-biblical liturgical rites which are not directly commanded in the New Testament.

Below, we have offered the Reformation Fellowship Free-Worship Liturgy for your review. It has, in our experience, served as a particularly fruitful structure for our network of biblical house churches. Our Sunday gathering template is available to download for free at ReformationFelllowship.org/Liturgy.

FREE-WORSHIP LITURGY OUTLINE

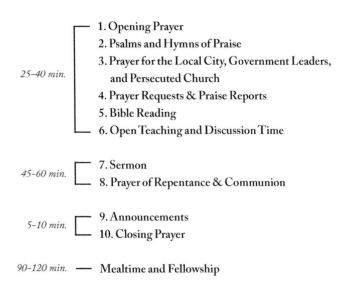

25-40 min.
1. Opening Prayer
2. Psalms and Hymns of Praise
3. Prayer for the Local City, Government Leaders, and Persecuted Church
4. Prayer Requests & Praise Reports
5. Bible Reading
6. Open Teaching and Discussion Time

45-60 min.
7. Sermon
8. Prayer of Repentance & Communion

5-10 min.
9. Announcements
10. Closing Prayer

90-120 min. — Mealtime and Fellowship

The following chapter provides a brief overview and biblical support for each portion of the Free-Worship Liturgy.

Free-Worship Liturgy
THE ORDER OF BIBLICAL WORSHIP

CALLING THE BODY TO COME TOGETHER
(1 Cor. 14:26; Heb. 10:25; 1 Cor. 11:17-18)

Conducted generally by an elder or by the man of the home in which the church is gathered, a verbal call to transition from informal fellowship to the formal meeting shall occur. The call to come together is a declaration to the body that the structure and roles of our common Christian life are about to transition to the structure and roles of ecclesiastical life. While this may seem strange to some, this principle is seen everywhere in the human experience. For example, a work environment shifts our behavior from private life to professional life. At home, we may be the leader, while at work, we may not. At home, we can act as we wish; in the boardroom, we must act according to our job description. Likewise, these transitioning conditions of conduct apply equally to the church.

This individual should continue by welcoming the congregation, acknowledging any guests, offering housekeeping exhortations or directions (location of bathrooms or where a parent can take a crying child), and quieting the room in preparation for prayer.

1. OPENING PRAYER

(Acts 2:42; Mark 11:24; 1 Thes. 5:17; Eph. 6:18)

Conducted either by the man of the home in which the church is gathered or by any other elder-appointed man to fulfill this duty. Opening prayers have no boundaries, but a prayer of thankfulness, blessing, and edification in regards to the assembled church should be in view.

2. PSALMS AND HYMNS OF PRAISE

(1 Cor. 14:26; Eph. 5:19; Ps. 100:1-4)

In accordance with the doctrines set forth in *Doctrines: Article 07*, a man appointed by the elder(s) of the church should lead the congregation in voice and/or by instrument in the singing of psalms or hymns of praise. Although a liturgy will list pre-planned songs, this shouldn't forbid spontaneous congregational suggestions for specific psalms or hymns during the meeting.

> **Suggestion:** We have found it fruitful but not mandatory for house churches to have hymnals and custom songbooks made from three-ring binders. Reformation Fellowship suggests the Hymns of Grace hymnal by The Master's Seminary Press and can be purchased at ReformationFellowship.org/Hymnal. Songbooks can house

any modern sheet music (not found in the hymnals) that the elders may believe to be edifying for the congregation.

3. PRAYER FOR THE LOCAL CITY, GOVERNMENT LEADERS, AND PERSECUTED CHURCH

(1 Tim. 2:1-4, Heb. 13:3)

The Christian's ability to freely enjoy Christian assembly and public worship are dependent upon the leaders of their land. The elder(s) are to select a man to lead the congregation in prayer for the ministry of the local city, the governing leaders (locally and nationally), and those Christians who live in a place of persecution due to the lack of righteous leaders in their land. This portion of the liturgy should offer members a reminder of the local and global mission of the Gospel, the importance of praying for those in power, and their brothers and sisters in Christ who live all over the world.

4. PRAYER REQUESTS AND PRAISE REPORTS

(1 Tim. 2:1-15; 1 Cor. 14:26; James 5:16; Acts 2:42:)

In accordance with *Doctrines: Article 06,* the elders should open up the meeting to members of the church for open participation from both men and women to submit prayer requests, personal needs, supplications, confessions, and praise of answered prayers. While this time is open to all, prayer should be performed by the men. This is an intimate and organic time that may include or lead to moments of beautiful, Spirit-led discussion and powerful prayer. However, this time may also include what can feel like awkward silence. Elders should be willing to endure these silent moments as it often takes time for more timid members to submit their requests. Furthermore, it is the elder(s) role to shepherd the flock gently through this time, keeping the discussion within the bounds of the liturgical focus without exhibiting a spirit of control.

5. BIBLE READING

(1 Tim. 4:13; 2 Tim 4:2; Acts 2:42; 2 Tim. 3:14-17; Rom. 10:17)

Scripture reading has always been central to the local church. In fact, St. Justin Martyr's *First Apology* written in A.D. 155 states, "And on the day called Sunday, all who live in cities or in the country gather together to one place, and the memoirs of the apostles or the writings of the prophets are read, as long as time permits…"[1] Therefore, the elder(s) should select a man to read aloud one full chapter of the Old or New Testament.

6. OPEN TEACHING AND DISCUSSION TIME

(1 Cor. 14:26-40; Eph. 4:11-16; 1 Tim. 4:13)

In a time where most church gatherings have been reduced to a mere monologue of one preacher, we believe an open teaching time offers the men an opportunity to explore and exercise their spiritual gifts and duties under the oversight of elders. Coming off the heels of the Bible reading portion of the liturgy, this time may simply be a short discussion of what was read, but it may also include personal testimonies, biblical illuminations, exhortations, short Scripture-based

---

1 Cyril C. Richardson. *Early Christian Fathers* (Louisville: Westminster John Knox Press, 1953).

teachings, and theological or doctrinal discussions.

7. SERMON

(1 Tim. 4:13; Jam. 3:1; 2 Tim. 3:16-17; 2 Tim. 4:2; Rom. 10:14-15; Rom. 1:15; 1 Cor. 1:18; Matt. 28:19-20; 2 Tim. 2:2; Col. 1:28-29; 1 Tim. 3:2; Gal. 6:6; Tit. 2:15; Acts 15:35)

In accordance with *Convictions: Articles 02-03*, the elder(s) of the church are to preach an expository sermon for the edification of the assembly. While the pulpit is to be filled first and foremost by the preaching of elders, sermons can and should also be delivered by those honorable men in the congregation who have been bestowed with the gift of teaching.

> **Suggestion:** We have found it fruitful but not mandatory for house churches to purchase a basic lectern, music stand, or wooden pulpit. This allows the preacher to separate from his family and children and stand with his Bible and notes in a place where all can easily see him and hear the content being presented.

8. A PRAYER OF REPENTANCE & COMMUNION

(Acts 2:42; 1 Cor. 11:27-32; 17-32; Matt. 3:8; Matt. 26:26-29; 1 John 1:9)

In preparation for communion, an elder or deacon should pray for the congregation, thank God for the forgiveness of sins we have through Christ, and lead the congregation into a time of silent prayer (1-2 minutes) where each member can have a moment to reflect, confess, and repent of any unacknowledged sin to God.

In accordance with our Statement on Communion, the elder or deacon should instruct the men to arise and retrieve the elements for themselves and their families and then wait for their instruction so they may partake in the Lord's Supper together with the entire church. The facilitator of communion is to take the elements in his hands, bring identification to the purpose of the elements in alignment with 1 Corinthians 11:17-32, thank God for both the bread and cup and instruct members to eat and drink collectively as families and jointly as a church. The elder(s) should consider offering an additional portion of time (approximately 1-2 minutes) for members to reflect on the meaning of this ordinance prior to proceeding.

9. ANNOUNCEMENTS

The elder(s) are to offer all members of the congregation a chance to share any announcements pertinent to the church (mid-week meetings, needs, planned absences, birthdays, etc.).

10. CLOSING PRAYER

(Acts 2:42; Mark 11:24; 1 Thes. 5:17; Eph. 6:18)

Either an elder or a man from the congregation is to close the formalized portion of the church gathering and thank God for the blessings delivered during the meeting and for the upcoming provisions of food, drink, and fellowship.

MEALTIME AND FELLOWSHIP

(Acts 2:42; Acts 2:46; Acts 20:7; 1 Cor. 10:31; Heb. 10:24-25)

Those familiar with the processes and consumer culture of the Western Church may be prone to divide the formal assembly from the informal assembly. That is, some may believe that the informal mealtime and fellowship are not part of the church liturgy. That is not true. In fact, Acts 2:42 states that Christians, "... continued steadfastly in the apostles' doctrine and fellowship, in the breaking of bread, and in prayers." We believe that experiencing fellowship through food offers a place of not only relational depth but also an opportunity for members to follow up with the needs, lessons, and ideas expressed during the formal assembly.

> **Suggestion:** In an effort to diversify the labor involved in cooking and cleaning, consider ordering your mealtime around an organized potluck. We have also found it fruitful to remind the congregation to each do their part in serving to restore the host home to a state of cleanliness before leaving. Lastly, hosting can be a demanding task; for that reason, we have found that relinquishing the host or hostess from contributing a potluck meal is a simple way to lighten their labors.

CONCLUSION

There are a latitude of church liturgies out there. However, we are to view them simply as a tool for local shepherds to build up the church in biblical truth. All church liturgies should be both edifying to the assembly and rooted in Scripture. While it may seem smart to add additional, extra-biblical elements to your church's liturgy, we must be sure to determine if it is right to do so. As we mentioned earlier in this handbook, God's intentionality and precise specifications for the building of His houses of worship declare His expectation to hold to His orders. May we never make *His* meeting *our* meeting. Amen.

 Download the Official Reformation Fellowship Free Worship Liturgy at: ReformationFellowship.org/Liturgy

CLOSING

For more information and resources about planting or strengthening a biblical house church, please visit ReformationFellowship.org or our church planting school at ReformationSeminary.com. This handbook can be purchased on our website. This manuscript was developed and copyrighted in 2020 by Reformation Fellowship (a companion ministry of Reformation Seminary). Written and edited by Dale Partridge. Further editing and review by the Reformation Seminary Theological Advisory Board. Publication Version 1.2.

FIND A HOUSE CHURCH

Point your phone's camera at the QR code below to be taken to the Reformation Fellowship house church locator.

BIBLIOGRAPHY

Listed in the order of appearance.

O'Brien, Brandon J. *The Strategically Small Church: Intimate, Nimble, Authentic, and Effective.* Bloomington, MN: Bethany House, 2010.

Koesel, Karrie J. *The Rise of a Chinese House Church: The Organizational Weapon,* The China Quarterly 215 (2013): 572–89. doi:10.1017/S0305741013000684.

Whitney, Donald S. *Spiritual Disciplines Within the Church.* Chicago: Moody, 1996.

Spurgeon, Charles. *Metropolitan Tabernacle Pulpit,* Volume 35. New York: Pilgrim Publishing, 1975.

Carter, Tom. *Charles Spurgeon at His Best*, Grand Rapids, MI: Baker, 1988.

Tozer, A.W. *Church*, Camp Hills, PA: Wingspread, 2019.

Muether, John. *Tabletalk Magazine*: *Knowing His Voice*, March 2009.

Kuiper, R.B. *The Glorious Body of Christ*, Grand Rapids: Eerdmans, 1996.

Grace Community Church. *What We Teach: The Doctrinal Statement of Grace Community Church.* https://www.grace church.org/about/doctrinal-statement

Brown, Scott. *A Weed in the Church,* Raleigh: Merchant Adventurers, 2011.

DeYoung, Kevin and Gilbert, Greg. *What is the Mission of the Church?*. Wheaton: Crossway, 2011.

Reeves, Stan. *The 1689 Baptist Confession of Faith in Modern English*. Cape Coral, FL: Founders Press, 2017.

Piper, John. *Biblical Eldership*. DesiringGod.org, www.desiringgod.org/messages/biblical-eldership-session-1.

MacArthur, John. *The Master's Plan for the Church*. Chicago: Moody Press, 1991.

Bainton, Roland H. *Here I Stand; A life of Martin Luther*. (New York: Mentor, 1950.

MacArthur, John. *Preaching: How to Preach Biblically*. Nashvhille: Thomas Nelson, 2005.

Chapel, Bryan. *Christ-Centered Preaching: Redeeming the Expository Sermon*. Ada Michigan: Baker Academic, 2005.

The Council on Biblical Manhood and Womanhood. *Danvers Statement*. Danvers, Massachusetts, December 1988, cbmw.org/about/danvers-statement.

Richardson, Cyril C. *Early Christian Fathers* (Louisville: Westminster John Knox Press, 1953).

Printed in Great Britain
by Amazon